My Now for the
Entrepreneur

My Now for the
Entrepreneur

Moovin4ward Publishing
Huntsville, Alabama

Copyright 2013 Moovin4ward Publishing

Library of Congress Control Number: 2013911344

ISBN: Paperback   978-0-9884564-64
       eBook   978-0-9884564-71

Printed in the United States of America

All rights reserved. No part of this publication may be reproduced, stored in a retrieval system or transmitted in any form or by any means, electronic, mechanical, photocopying, recording or otherwise, without the written permission of the publisher.

Publisher:
    Moovin4ward Publishing
    A Division of Moovin4ward Presentations LLC
    www.Moovin4ward.com

Contents

Part 1: Passion & Purpose 7
Step Out on Faith and Keep On Stepping 9
Do More than Dream 21
You Don't Have to Do It Alone 31
It's Just the Entrepreneur in Me 41
The Business of You 53

Part 2: Preparation & Planning 61
Stop, Drop & Roll 63
When a Deck is Not a Deck 71
Prerequisites to Entrepreneurial You 85
Making Lemons into Lemon Margaritas 99
What's Your Burger? 121

Part 3: Process & Practice 135
How to Defeat the Enemies of Entrepreneurship 137
From Bedsides to Beads 151
The Right Stuff 159
Let's Make A Deal to Not Chase the Deal 173
Ready, Aim, Fire 187
Quiet Resilience 199

My Now…

...for the Entrepreneur

Part 1: Passion & Purpose

My Now...

Marcie Hill

Marcie Hill, M.S., is an entrepreneur, blogger, author, and speaker who stepped out on faith to pursue her passion of writing. In 2008, she ditched the life jackets of paychecks and benefits to jump into the unknown waters of writing, blogging and publishing.

Along her journey, she discovered the lack of value placed on writing and critical thinking in the American school system which ultimately results in the poor quality of writing and a lack of original thoughts and creativity in society. She is currently on a mission to revolutionize the art of writing by teaching students how to integrate writing, technology and creativity to produce amazing literary and individual expressionistic works of art.

Email: msmarcie@marciewrites.com

Website: www.marciewrites.com

Twitter: marcie_hill

LinkedIn: marciehill

...for the Entrepreneur

Step Out on Faith and Keep On Stepping

Marcie Hill

Your faith walk is one of the hardest things that you will experience in your life. Hebrews 11:1 says, "Now faith is being sure of what we hope for and certain of what we do not see." This means, you have to work hard and move forward _knowing_ that something great is going to happen; but you don't know when or how it will happen.

In February 2008, I stepped out on faith and left my job and 12-year career in human resources to pursue my dreams of being a magazine writer. I had no solid plan; I just had visions of seeing my name gracing the bylines in *Essence*, *Chicago*, *Parade*, *Black Enterprise* and *Entrepreneur* magazines.

The early stages of my writing journey brought more rejections and disappointments than successes, which made it very easy to actively pursue my distractions of blogging and social media. Both were a blessing and a curse at the same time. While it was great learning about this new technology, I took my eyes off my prize of writing for publications. But I kept stepping forward in faith.... without a plan.

It is five years later and my vision has grown since I took that initial step on my faith walk. While being a magazine writer is still on my radar, my dreams have grown to include writing and blogging for corporations, professional speaking and teaching people writing skills through blogging. Thus, I am on a mission to use my skills, gifts and abilities to serve others while making my writing, blogging and speaking dreams come true...with a plan.

Over the years, I discovered at least 10 actions that **must** be taken or qualities you **must** possess that are essential for a successful faith walk. **Warning: this walk is neither quick nor easy.** But it's totally necessary to realize your full potential, to work your purpose and to reach your dreams.

1. <u>Prayer</u>

Daily prayer is essential. I begin each day by asking God what I should be doing, because what I want to do may not be aligned with His plan for me. I also ask for focus, direction, divine connections, and favor.

Focus keeps your attention on the task at hand. Even when you get sidetracked by distractions around you, focus will get you back on point. Direction keeps you moving forward on the path of completion. The people placed in your life to help you accomplish your goals and reach your dreams are divine connections. Favor is God's blessing upon your life.

Keep in mind that people come into your life for a reason, a season or a lifetime. The people who are there for a reason or season may disappear after their mission is accomplished. There is no need to develop or harbor ill feelings; just know that their work in your life is done. Thank God for the help and lessons learned and move on.

2. Courage

Getting starting is the hardest part of any venture, and you will have to make bold, crazy moves to achieve your dream. While it is courageous to take the first on your faith walk, you have to continue to step boldly in faith. While it takes courage to ask for help, you have to be bold to ask a complete stranger for assistance. Moreover, you will have to do things you have never thought about doing.

When I left my job, I was excited and afraid. I was leaving the security of a consistent paycheck and benefits to venture into the unknown world of writing. I had a lot to learn, so I started reaching out to people I didn't know to gain information. The fact that many of them were generous with their time and advice gave me the courage to continue to reach out to professional strangers and do other things I had never done before.

My Now...

My most courageous act to date was requesting an interview with Dr. Maya Angelou. When I sent the message asking for an interview, I honestly didn't think I would get a response. Imagine my amazement and excitement when my interview was granted and I was speaking with this living legend within two weeks! This was a very humbling experience and a big huge blessing. The biggest blessing of all, though, was seeing our interview published on her birthday in *St. Louis Magazine*, a major publication in her hometown.

3. Determination

You have to have dogged determination on your faith walk. You have to want your dream so badly that you will do what you have to do to see it come to life despite obstacles and challenges. When the storms of life blow and shake up your smooth flow, you may have to change directions or even stop temporarily. As long as you keep your eyes and mind on your prize, you will continue on your journey after the storms blow over.

Even though I am not where I want to be in my life right now, I have strong resolve to see my dreams come to life. I refuse to quit. In fact, I cannot afford to stop as I have invested too much time, money and energy.

4. Plan of Action

"When you fail to plan, you plan to fail." You **have** to have a plan of action. It doesn't have to be 50 pages but it must state what you want to accomplish, the steps that must be taken and an "ideal" completion date. After you write down your plan, you have to set goals. A goal is a dream with a completion date. Most importantly, you have to have money saved.

I failed at this on two fronts. First, I just knew my plan A was going to work so I did not have a plan B. Remember, my plan A wasn't solid in the first place. And when the money ran out, I was a wreck. My friends became the First National Bank of Marcie. While it was a blessing to have people on which I could call in case of emergencies, it was a horrible feeling *to have* to ask people for money when you are an able-bodied, gifted individual.

As with any journey there will bumps, twists and turns, cul-de-sacs and detours. You will succeed as long as you endure.

5. Belief in Possibilities

You know the desires of your heart, but do you *really* believe you can have them? Many people don't, which is why they never begin to pursue their dreams. Here's the reality of making your dreams come true: when you put energy behind any action, the Universe responds. In fact, your initial vision will magnify and more opportunities will appear. Things you would have never dreamt possible will begin to happen and manifest. Just know that you can have everything you want if you *truly* believe you can have it.

There are two ways to increase your belief in your dreams: write them down and create a vision board. Things become real when you write them down because an abstract concept is being transformed into a physical form.

However, your dreams become even more vivid when you create a vision board because you are actually seeing the desires of your heart.

6. Patience

The dictionary defines patient as "bearing pain or trials without complaint; showing self-control; calm; steadfast." Patience is essential to achieving everything you want because your timing is not God's timing, and everything happens in divine order. Thus, you may compromise your dream if you move too fast, too slow or not at all.

Patience is also a great character builder. You will no longer react to small people with small thoughts doing small things. You will become very resourceful and a great listener. Most importantly, you will gain a lot of wisdom.

...for the Entrepreneur

Mark Cuban, one of the billionaires on the reality TV show, *Shark Tank*, told an entrepreneur, "It takes 10 to 15 years to become an overnight success." Do you have the patience to wait that long to make your dreams come true?

7. <u>Work</u>

You can have all the dreams you want but nothing will happen if you don't make a move. Work is what activates your dream. The bible says that faith without works is dead. Therefore, only when you put forth an effort will things begin to happen.

Ideally, you will do something each day to move closer to achieving your goals – read an article, send an e-mail, make a phone call or research a topic. You should also check your goal dates often so you can establish a track record of completion.

I write every day. This helps me to establish a pattern of writing frequently; it improves my abilities; and it enhances my creativity. It also boosts my confidence, which makes it easier for me to promote myself and my services.

Thomas Edison said, "Opportunity is missed by most people because it is dressed in overalls and looks like work." Don't let this be you.

8. Support from others

On your faith walk, you will have cheerleaders, encouragers, mentors, coaches and strangers that genuinely care about your success. In fact, you need these people because they are the wind beneath your wings. Some of them may not have your ambition; many of them will have no idea what your profession is; but they will make sure that you get to your destination.

Your supporters may be people you know personally; other people will "adopt" you because they admire your drive; still, your persistence and enthusiasm will attract others. No matter how you gain your "fans", be sure to always say "thank you".

Just knowing that people are genuinely concerned about your progress and success makes it easier to move forward. An encouraging word, an inspirational text message or a "thinking of you" e-mail means a lot on the lonely road to success and dream attainment.

9. Focus

There is an overused term these days called "laser focus", which means to really zero in on something. Essentially, whatever has your attention is what will produce the greatest results. There are six ways you can focus to ensure your dreams come true:

- Avoid or minimize distractions
- Tune out negative people
- Turn off negative self-talk and self-doubt
- Revolve decisions and actions around your dreams and goals
- Keep your eyes on the prize
- Practice patience and faith

10. <u>Persistence</u>

You must NEVER give up. This is the hardest part of your journey because giving up is so easy to do. Honestly, never starting and giving up are the easiest – and worst - things that you can do. Following are a few quotes for you to reference when you get discouraged and want to quit.

Nothing in this world can take the place of persistence. Talent will not; nothing is more common than unsuccessful people with talent. Genius will not; unrewarded genius is almost a proverb. Education will not; the world is full of educated failures. Persistence and determination alone are omnipotent. - Calvin Coolidge

Patience, persistence and perspiration make an unbeatable combination for success. - Napoleon Hill

Success is almost totally dependent upon drive and persistence. The extra energy required to make another effort

My Now...

or try another approach is the secret of winning. - Denis Waitley

Ambition is the path to success, persistence is the vehicle you arrive in. - William Eardley IV

****

I started my journey in 2008 and have yet to see the huge results I desire. Believe me, I have thought about giving up several times but the following things have kept me going.

1. The support of people who care about me is amazing.
2. My small successes are stepping stones to my bigger dreams.
3. The thought of working for somebody for the rest of my life is not appealing on any level.
4. A JOB means "just over broke," and it's a bad feeling to swap time for dollars and still be underpaid.
5. I truly believe that the desires of my heart will manifest in ways that my human mind cannot fathom.

As a spiritual being having a human experience, it is never a good feeling to work every day and not see the results you desire, especially when the bills are due. However, it is imperative that you move forward, because if you stop, nothing is going to happen. Only when you put forth energy will the Universe respond.

What do you do when you have prayed, worked and did everything you know to do and still nothing happens?

Press forward with determination and enthusiasm knowing that you **will** see your dreams if you are bold, courageous and patient. And keep on working, praying and stepping in faith.

My Now...

Jonathan Oliver

Jonathan believes that life is what we are born with; living is what we do with it. His mission is to create a world of truth, love, and faith by helping individuals to harness their gifts and talents. He earned a Bachelor of Behavioral Science in 2003 majoring in Psychology, with a minor in Biology. He is the founder of Higher Enlightenment which he started in 2005. Higher Enlightenment is a firm that provides spiritual and intelligent insight to others which helps them to believe in themselves and reach beyond their fears.

Jonathan is a dynamic speaker and has presented a variety of programs to over 6000,000 people. He is also the author of *Impersonations,* which was released in 2009. It is an inspirational book that shares how he overcame dyslexia and a recovery program to live his dream.

Jonathan is a certified speaker for Rachel's Challenge, an organization committed to inspire, equip, and empower every person to create a permanent positive culture of change in their schools, businesses, and communities by starting a chain reaction of kindness and compassion.

...for the Entrepreneur

Do More than Dream
Jonathan Oliver

An addict will tell you they have dreamed of one day being clean and sober. It doesn't matter what the addiction: food, sex, crack, alcohol, gambling, or shopping. A person who is in recovery and is clean and sober will tell you that dream was only the beginning, but not enough. They need more than a dream. Trust me, I know. I'm speaking from real life experiences. I have been in recovery from having an addiction to pornography since October 2003. In the bible faith is defined as "the substance of things hoped for, the evidence of things not seen" (Hebrews 11:1 KJV). God still requires more. The dream has been argued to be the most important part of having an entrepreneur spirit.

Wikipedia defines entrepreneur as a loaned word from French, and is commonly used to describe an individual who organizes and operates a business or businesses, taking on financial risk to do so. Webster defines entrepreneur as one who organizes, manages, and assumes the risks of a business or enterprise. In both definitions something is being implied...ACTION.

My Now...

While we are defining things, let's touch on what's not being said but is definitely being felt...FEAR. The fear of losing everything and looking like a fool. The fear of getting it wrong. The fear of embarrassment.

Every year I make a list of goals. Here is my list for 2013.

S.M.A.R.T. Goals in 2013

1) Trust Jesus-find a church home, repent, accept forgiveness, ask for help, and praise His name.
2) Attend one SAA meeting a month, including from the road.
3) Magnified Saran-honesty, spoiling her, and couple activities.
4) Read two chapters a week on Failing Forward until the book is finished.
5) Write one chapter a month or ten pages each until the book is finished.
6) Lose 1 pound a week until 40 pounds have been lost.
7) Go to a workout class when on the road.
8) Speak internationally.
9) Pay off old and new taxes.
10) Strengthen my relationships with my: Father, Brothers, Niece, and Nephews.
11) Go to Napa Valley, Ca.
12) Enter a cycling race.

13) Get an iPhone 4s or 5.
14) Video tape a new speech a month.
15) Review S.M.A.R.T. Goals in 2013 every Sunday.
16) Be willing to fail, make a mistake, get it wrong, look stupid, but be willing to TRY!!!!

"Knowing others is wisdom; knowing yourself is enlightenment"--Tao Te Ching

S.M.A.R.T. Goals are specific, measurable, attainable, relevant, and timely. They say, "You want to make God laugh? Make plans." I like to say, "You want to see God's plans? Start laughing..." In Jeremiah 29:11(CEM) it is written "I know the plans I have in mind for you, declares the Lord; they are plans for peace, not disaster, to give you a future filled with hope.

It's the risk that makes someone an entrepreneur. There are billions of people on the planet and there may be some people that even share the same name as you. However there is only one YOU. Why not bank on being the best you ever? It's fair to say most people know Oprah Winfrey. Winfrey was called "arguably the world's most powerful woman" by CNN and Time.com, "arguably the most influential woman in the world" by the American Spectator, "one of the 100 people who most influenced the 20th Century", and "one of the most influential people" from 2004 to 2011 by TIME.

My Now...

Forbes' international rich list has listed Winfrey as the world's only black billionaire from 2004 to 2006 and as the first black woman billionaire in world history. According to Forbes, in September 2010 Winfrey was worth over $2.7 billion and has overtaken former eBay CEO Meg Whitman as the richest self-made woman in America. Let us start from the beginning. Winfrey is best known for her self-titled, multi-award-winning talk show "The Oprah Winfrey Show" which was the highest-rated program of its kind in history and was nationally syndicated from 1986 to 2011.

Books have been written about the greatness of Oprah Winfrey, but let me go even farther back. Before The Oprah Winfrey Show was a major hit, Winfrey was presented by her lawyer with a choice. It was very simple. To either sign a contract to where the network would pay her or to setup a contract that allowed her to pay herself based on how well the show was doing. That was the choice on the table: allow the network to set your salary or pay yourself a salary. The risk was if the network paid her salary and the show was doing amazing then she could lose potential earnings because she would be locked into this contract with the network. But, on the other hand, if the show was doing badly she would still be making her same salary without risking any income. Winfrey's lawyer advised her to set up a contract that allowed her to pay herself based on how well the show was doing.

...for the *Entrepreneur*

Winfrey thought about it and agreed. Her reasoning was who better to bank on yourself other than you. She said "There is only one Oprah Winfrey and no one on earth can do a better job at being me than me". What a powerful statement. Possibly make millions or even billions, or have a safe and comfortable salary. Winfrey took the risk and the rest as they say is history.

Why not bet on you? Then, become the best you that you can ever become. What's the worst that can happen? You fail. Failing may be a good thing. Restaurateur Wolfgang Puck says, "I learned more from the one restaurant that didn't work than from all the ones that were successes." This is a guy that knows a thing or two about success. Considering he owns five critically acclaimed restaurants in California-Spago, Chinois on Main, Postrio, the Eureka Brewery, and Granita-not to mention he has also opened restaurants in Chicago, Las Vegas, and Tokyo. John C. Maxwell, one of my all-time favorite authors, wrote in his book "Failing Forward" the road to the next level is always uphill, so you can't coast there. This is a book I highly recommend you read if you are serious about becoming an entrepreneur. Because you will never know who you are and what you are until you've really been tested.

Business author Jim writes, "Contrary to popular belief, I consider failure a necessity in business. If you're not failing at least five times a day, you're probably not doing enough".

My Now...

You may be saying to yourself, Jonathan that sounds all and good, but its Oprah Winfrey for goodness sake. I can't even relate to being on that level. Well let me share with you a little bit about Jonathan Oliver. Since I was a little boy my grandmother has always told me to shoot for the moon and reach the stars.

When I graduated from Hardin-Simmons University in Abilene, TX, I was shooting for the stars. I had been accepted to medical school. I had been part of four Division III conference football championships in a row. The world was my oyster. My parents, family, and friends all spoke highly about me getting into medical school and one day becoming an orthopedic surgeon. I had been shadowing doctors in undergrad for four years. I had racked up over 600 volunteer hours during that time. However my absolute passion was to become a motivational speaker and one day, a published author. I had been team captain in high school and college. While in college I had several leadership positions and never shyed away from public speaking.

As I got closer to attending medical school, the more I was being torn in two different directions. One part of me was saying becoming a doctor would open more doors for me and allow me to be more creditable as a motivational speaker. Not to mention I would be young, single, and financially successful. I also knew deep down I had the worst attitude and reasoning for wanting to become a doctor. Sex,

...for the Entrepreneur

power, and wealth. The funny part was I wanted to become a motivational speaker to help people. That was my dream.

Becoming a motivational speaker had more unknowns. I had no idea where to begin. Pursuing a career as a doctor wasn't by any means easier, but the blueprint was more structured: medical school, residency, and fellowship. Becoming a motivational speaker was not as structured. Plus I am dyslexic and I find reading and writing to be very difficult most of the time and not fun. I struggled in high school but still graduated with honors. I also struggled in college. So why would I purposefully put myself on this path? Why would I want to feel like I was in a dark room with a very small flashlight searching for pieces of a puzzle?

In that moment, two months before starting medical school, I made a choice. Why go the long way around the mountain if I knew in the depths of my heart that I wanted to be a motivational speaker? I decided to take the risk. I started out by getting a part time job waiting tables. I made a list of people who I felt could help answer questions I needed answered. I spoke with my pastor and others. I was advised to join a Toastmasters Club. The club has two objectives; help you face your fear of public speaking and to help one become a better speaker. I used it for the latter. Over the next two years, I would work my way up becoming a manager at the restaurant I worked for and began working on my first book. I would also get my first speaking

My Now...

engagement. It was for F.C.A (Fellow Christian Athletes). I still remember my first speech, "Suffering to become stronger." I would then move to be closer to my then girlfriend and now wife. She is a doctor and on her way to becoming a cardiologist. All journeys and choices don't end in failure. I believe my true purpose at the time of me pursing becoming a doctor wasn't to become a doctor... It was to meet my wife. There are treasures on all paths if we keep our eyes and heart open to receiving them.

From to 2004-2013 my risk of wanting to follow my dream of becoming a motivational speaker and published author would lead me down a path of getting t-shirts, hugs, and coffee mugs as forms of payment for my presentations. My side jobs went from waiting tables to managing the restaurant, then back to waiting tables. I went from competing in speaking competitions with Toastmasters to having a contract with company through Monster World Wide to travel the country and speak to students about their academic and financial future. I would sleep in my car at times while traveling during the economic recession. But that's how strongly I believed in my dream.

During that time I owned my company, Higher Enlightenment. and was still writing my first book. I was fighting with stopping, struggling, and pushing through the frustration of thinking I was never going to finish that first book...but I did!!! I finally finished and became a published author. My first book "Impersonations" was now a reality.

Present day, I'm working on my second solo book and have collaborated on two others. I'm also a national speaker for an organization called Rachel's Challenge, which motivates students in the areas of kindness, compassion, and character development. I have worked my way up from 20 presentations a year to over 200. I have gone from speaking to audiences of 20 to now audiences of 2,000. Over the last 9 years, I have presented to almost 2 million people both domestic and internationally.

I'm no Oprah Winfrey, but I'm going to be the best Jonathan James Oliver I can be. I took the risk. I can say my worst day doing what I love is better than most people's best day doing what they hate. It's only the beginning and I don't have all the answers laid out in front of me. But I now have a solid structure and a good foundation. Taking that risk is one of the best choices I have ever made. It's good to dream, but dreams come true when you have the will to do more than just dream.

My Now...

Jenn Crenshaw

Jenn Crenshaw is the Chief Human Resources Officer for New Signature in Washington, DC. She specializes in designing and managing systems in talent acquisition, talent development, total rewards and internal communications & culture. Jenn joined New Signature from Burger King Corporation where she served as the VP of HR for North America. Her passion is in guiding the creation of the right organizational conditions and capacities for everyone to thrive and drive individual, team and company success. Jenn is a frequent speaker at professional events and conferences world-wide. She holds a Master of Science in Human Organizational Development from Villanova University and has been certified as a Senior Professional in Human Resources by the Society of Human Resource Management since 1999. Additionally, Jenn is an entrepreneur and co-owner of GlobeHopper Coffeehouse & Lounge in Richmond, VA.

...for the Entrepreneur

You Don't Have to Do It Alone

Jenn Crenshaw

I think most entrepreneurs and small business people will remember the Mitt Romney campaign commercial in 2012, the ones that profiled small business owners reacting to President Obama's comment that small business owners have not built their business alone. I won't comment on the political message of those commercials, however, I have to admit that I agree that no one builds a business alone. Whether your help and encouragement is coming from members of your family, members of your community or your business heroes; you are not in this alone. Some of your helpers along your journey may even be people you've never met in person. You may read your favorite blogger at just the right time; a friend may recount an experience they had that inspires you to take action. Encouragement, support and help are all there for you – they always have been for me.

It is my hope that you will find encouragement to take initiative and risk as you read about just a few of the lessons I learned growing up the child of an entrepreneur. I want to

My Now...

introduce you to my greatest teacher, helper and hero - my dad, Duane Catlett. Dad is a successful business man who will never have a fancy framed degree, who will always speak with less than perfect grammar and who will continue to have little interest in what happens on Wall Street. He is much more interested in what happens on Main Street. Dad's journey provided for me the lessons I have come to consider my real life MBA. I was taught lessons of economics, lessons of customer service and lessons of faith, hard work and generosity. I am a successful entrepreneur and human resources executive today because of what I learned from my parents. Together they've operated as many as eight dry cleaning stores over the past 45 years. Dad still enjoys working and continues to have a passion for his business. At the height of his business success others might have hired an operations manager so they could work less and spend their time on other pursuits; he never seriously considered that option. When I asked him why he gave me the same reason that he gives today regarding retirement – he still enjoys going to work and if he didn't have to work he would be spending money attending car shows– requiring him to return to work to fund his hobby. I remember distinctly dad saying to me "if you need more money you'll have to find more work". There were many economic lessons along the way; he always took the time to explain how business worked just experiencing everyday life like shopping or having dinner. One restaurant where we ate once a week provided baskets

...for the Entrepreneur

of hot bread, dad taught me that while I believed the bread was free the cost was actually built in to the cost of our meal. Nothing is free. Some costs may not be obvious at first but they are a fact none the less. I learned to calculate percentages in my head while shopping at JC Penney. He would say, "If that is marked down 30%, what is the new price?" I'd come home from shopping trips with mom proud of how much we had saved – dad would then give me a lesson in retail mark-up. Explaining that while he was proud that I wanted to save money, the owner of the store likely added 300% to their wholesale cost so I had still paid much more for my clothes than they were worth to the manufacturer. Over the years he seized every teachable moment to show me how to look at life as a business opportunity. He taught me by example that with hard work you can build a business and a great life for your family. Dad will be 69 years old this year and he continues to work 60 hours a week, he's not ready to retire work provides him with enjoyment and fulfillment.

Dad learned about hard work from his family. They were farmers and loggers – work that required long days and could be dangerous. In 1959, my grandfather was killed in a lumbering accident and dad became the man of the house at age 15, he completed high school while working in the local fruit orchards and with his uncles, hauling lumber. In the early 1960's, dad went to work for Corning Glass Company

My Now...

where he became a night shift supervisor. He knew pretty quickly that he was not built to punch a time clock. He wanted more. He was willing to take initiative and to take risks – he may not have known the term entrepreneur, never the less he was driven to strike out on his own. His dream was to own a filling station and garage – his passion has always been American muscle cars. It was the mid 1960's and the changes in the EPA's regulations for underground fuel tanks made buying the garage just out of reach financially. He and a couple friends leased a station for a short time but could not raise the capital to replace the underground tanks as required with a change in ownership. He may have been discouraged but he was not willing to give up. He had saved $1200 and was looking for a business opportunity that would free him from the hot and dirty, glass manufacturing job. He answered an advertisement in the classified section of the Martinsburg Journal. The founder, proprietor and franchisor of Nu-Look 1 HR Cleaners was willing to take on an apprentice. After spending 6 months learning the dry cleaning business working alongside Karl Dickey, dad opened his first of eight Nu-Look 1 HR Cleaners in Martinsburg, WV in 1968. It was this apprenticeship that gave my dad, a disadvantaged young man from a rural community an opportunity to realize his dreams. A stranger took a risk, and that risk paid off for everyone involved. Dad helped Mr. Dickey build his dream of franchising and my dad earned an opportunity that would have otherwise not been possible for a young man who had

...for the Entrepreneur

to start taking care of his family at 15 years of age. I am pleased that today there are programs such as Year Up and Urban Alliance providing internship and apprenticeship opportunities to young adults – many of them just like my dad, on the more difficult side of the opportunity divide. In 1993, I started my apprenticeship with my dad. It was the summer between my junior and senior year of college he partnered with me to open his newest business – a retail embroidery shop. He taught me how to launch a business and he supported me as I stumbled and made plenty of mistakes. I was two semesters short of earning my bachelor's degree and I was in an MBA level apprenticeship. I learned to operate a computerized embroidery machine, negotiate wholesale contracts and I marshaled the courage to go out and ask for sales. I was only able to do those things because I had the support of a business professional that taught me and supported me even when it was clear that I did not know what I was doing. He took a risk on me and I am fairly certain that today he believes that risk is paying off. I have learned from Mr. Dickey and my dad that no one can make it out here alone. I strive to continue to take risks on people and invest in their growth in the same way that Mr. Dickey invested in dad and dad invested in me.

Over the years, I watched as my family supported other small businesses with our buying habits and purchases. Preferring to buy groceries at an IGA (independent grocers association) store versus the large chain and hiring self-employed tradesmen to build decks, detail cars and repair steam presses and boilers. In the 1980's, there was a Nu-Look 1 HR Cleaner's franchisee who was struggling. Mr. Dickey approached my parents and asked them to buy out the other owner. My parents had four stores at that time and growth was expensive. The business was stable but adding this additional location was not going to be easy. It would have been easier to walk away and honestly that is probably what mom wanted to do. My dad wanted to help the other owner; he wanted to help him get out of a difficult situation. There was going to be upside for my parents in the long run for sure, the location is currently their most profitable, but at the time it was not the easy thing to do. Again, Dad took a risk driven mostly by his desire to help someone else even though it was not convenient for him. A little more than 10 years ago, my parents wanted to sell a couple of their locations. They found a buyer, however the buyer was unable to secure traditional financing. It was a young business man who was trying to grow his business, much in the way my parents had been 30 years earlier. My parents made the decision to finance the deal themselves. The next several years were tough as that young business man was often several months behind on his payments. My parents could have repossessed the two locations, they didn't. They were supportive and most would say generous. Because they were patient it worked out in the end. I learned from watching my parents that being rich, being wealthy is not about how much money you can save or stock pile it's about being generous. I learned from them to be generous with my money, my time, with my skills and my talents.

The attribute dad possesses that I find the most difficult to emulate is perseverance. I don't know if he realized in 1968 that 45 years later he would still be working in his dry cleaning stores six days a week 52 weeks a year. I don't think he can tell you the last time he took a full week off work. If I had to guess, I'd say it was due to a surgery back in the mid 1980's. He's definitely playing the long game. He didn't take a job to work for two or three years and then move on to something more challenging or exciting. He didn't set a goal of owning the stores for 5 years to flip them and make a profit and move on to something new and more interesting. I have always known that perseverance does not come as naturally to me as it seems to for my dad. My story up until now would be one of making a job change every couple of years. As I compare my own choices with my dad's I realize that I often go into a business opportunity, whether it be a start-up or a career move, with an exit strategy in mind. All the books on writing business plans recommend that you plan your exit strategy while planning for start-up and growth. I bought into that idea and many times talked to dad about his exit strategy. The truth is he doesn't have one. He will continue to run his business six days a week until he can't any longer.

My Now...

Sheryl Sandberg recently wrote the book, <u>Lean In</u> where she encourages young professionals not to make decisions about their career until they are actually faced with the decision. Good advice that I need to learn to take from Ms. Sandberg and from the example dad has set. One day he will know that it is time to make a different decision and he will. Until then he will persevere just as he has for 45 years. I am hopeful I will learn to do the same. I don't think it's a coincidence that as a young woman I chose a life verse: Philippians 3:12-14 "I'm not saying that I have this all together, that I have it made. But I am well on my way, reaching out for Christ, who has so wondrously reached out for me. Friends, don't get me wrong: By no means do I count myself an expert in all of this, but I've got my eye on the goal, where God is beckoning us onward—to Jesus. I'm off and running and I'm not turning back." (The Message)

I feel an overwhelming sense of responsibility to carry on the legacy lived out in front of me by my parents; a sense of responsibility to work hard, to be generous, and to persevere, especially when it's difficult, and tedious. Yes, we should all be doing work that we love, work we are passionate about – if you're not, quit. I used to believe that being an entrepreneur was an alternative to staying in the same job for 25 years. I realize now that most highly successful entrepreneurs have a process, a formula; rarely is their path of success random. They plan, they practice, they fail, they succeed, and they keep going.

...for the *Entrepreneur*

Where ever your entrepreneurial dream takes you I hope you will remember you don't have to do it alone.

My Now...

Andrea Foy

Andrea Foy is an award-winning international author, speaker, consultant and coach. She conducts workshops and seminars on topics such as: Women's Issues, Business Skills, Diversity, Image Consulting, Personal Success Strategic Plan and the Hire Power Series. Andrea is a Certified Professional Coach, a Certified Diversity Training Consultant and a Certified Facilitator with Moovin4ward Presentations. She is also an Independent John Maxwell Leadership Coach.

You can reach Andrea at **info@andreafoy.com** or visit her website at **www.andreafoy.com**.

...for the *Entrepreneur*

It's Just the Entrepreneur in Me
Andrea Foy

Derived from the Old French word **entreprendre**, or *to undertake*; see enterprise, an entrepreneur is a person who "a person who organizes and manages any enterprise, especially a business, usually with considerable initiative and risk or an employer of productive labor; contractor." (Dictionary.com) According to Merriman.com, an entrepreneur is "one who organizes, manages, and assumes the risks of a business or enterprise." (Merriman.com)

Enterprise

1. a project undertaken or to be undertaken, especially one that is important or difficult or that requires boldness or energy; 2. a plan for such a project; 3. participation or engagement in such projects: Our country was formed by the enterprise of resolute men and women; 4. boldness or readiness in undertaking; adventurous spirit; ingenuity. 5. a company organized for commercial purposes; business firm.

My Now...

I included the definition for enterprise because as I researched my family history for this chapter, words like enterprise, innovative, focus, goals, saving, determination, vision, boldness, etc. kept coming to mind. Our country was formed by the enterprise of resolute men and women and because of Jim Crow and segregation laws enforced by local governments, a lot of African American goals were never noted and accomplishments went unnoticed.

Family History

I had always heard about my family's success and their achievements, but it wasn't until actually talking to my family about this book, that I actually began to really see that I inherited strong entrepreneurial skills. Now I do have firefighters, military, government, teachers, college professors, doctors and the like in my family who were very successful, but the nucleus of the family were the innovative risk takers; the essence of entrepreneurship.

Paternal Family Efforts

My dad had a hard upbringing in NC. Alonza Foy grew up on a farm, working day after day, morning to night, all year long, so hard in fact that at the age of 17, right after high school graduation and a few weeks shy of his 18th birthday, my dad enlisted in the Air Force. He just wanted out

...for the Entrepreneur

of his small town of less than 10,000 people, that didn't offer young black men any hope of doing much other than farming. He never looked back. The Air Force took him all over the world, even to Vietnam. He served 20 years. I have many other military relatives as well.

My father was always an entrepreneur. I never found out when and where he picked up the entrepreneur bug. It was always a part of my life with him and I guess I absorbed it from him and several other members of my family.

While serving in the Air Force, he opened a travel bag and upholstery shop. He recovered old sofas and chairs and also made vinyl garment bags for people to travel with. He was very successful. He started in our garage, at one point he owned a store front on the main street of the suburb near the military base where we lived. He was the only Black business owner in the town and got front page recognition by the local paper at the time.

He tried his best to make me, my cousins and brother work in the business over the years but as adolescents, we weren't having any of it. Youth is wasted on the young, had I known then what I know now I would have jumped at the chance to learn about the business and would have done all I could. Something must have rubbed off though because I inherited the entrepreneur DNA of the family.

My Now...

Later in life, my dad sold laptops, almost door-to-door style, before they were a household name. When laptops were first invented he joined a company that allowed him to buy them at wholesale and sell retail. He did really well until they began to appear in stores.

He bought empty vans and "pimped" them out way before the TV reality shows. The vans would literally have two seats in them and nothing else. He would carpet them, buy seats, put in TV's and have an antenna on top, lighting, CB's you name it; he could get it in a van. He was very creative. He received many offers to customize vans for others but he only tried a few and sold them. It was very time consuming, I would still watch in amazement... absorbing.

His efforts allowed my Mom to be a stay-at-home-mom and afforded us to still live a middle-income existence. He was always doing something on the side.

In his later life, Alonza developed a graphics shop, again in his home: Designing church programs and filming special church events for DVDs. He was also a photographer.

Along the way he never hesitated to call me to help him. I learned so much from just helping out with photography for a wedding, putting a church program together, etc. As I got old enough, I began to slowly realize he might be onto something and enjoyed the benefits derived from the extra

...for the Entrepreneur

money he was making and realized that I wanted to do things like this instead of that 9 to 5, 30 year retirement route.

As a matter of fact, several members on the paternal side of my family all were budding entrepreneurs to various degrees. An uncle owned a used car lot for a while, they all have the talent and ability to sew, upholster, manicure, they have been wedding planners, etc. They keep busy with something new all of the time. They are the artistic, creative side of me.

<u>Entrepreneurs come up with new ideas, innovations, and products, as well as construct creative, strategic marketing plans.</u>

Maternal Family Efforts

Charlie McKoy was in essence the perfect entrepreneur; he was a farmer by trade. My late grandfather on my mother's side was one of the first black land owners in a small North Carolina town in the 1930s. He owned over 100 acres of land, he worked hard to keep. He grew and sold mostly cotton and tobacco. He raised nine children on the farm, including my mom. Charlie had to feed his family of 10 and in the 1940s and 50s that was not easy to do for a black man in rural south. Some of the entrepreneurial efforts, my granddad employed were:

My Now...

In the early 30s, my grandfather bought a car. Instead of using the money from the farm to pay it off, he paid if off by driving workers to the nearby military base Ft. Bragg, which was 30 miles away, so that they could work on the base. He would go get them after work as well. Without him, most people could not afford to take a taxi to and from the base and could not afford a car and gas, which inhibited them from the civilian government jobs that paid so well for their families back then.

He bought farm equipment and to help pay for farm expenses, he rented it out to other farmers who couldn't afford to finance their own farm equipment, so they could still benefit from the newest equipment and technologies and make money for their families.

When it was time to harvest crops, he would listen to the radio and find out when the markets were peaking and hire what we call now day labors, (hands) to quickly bring the crops in while they were at their peak as well as when the market was high to receive the highest price for his crops.

The Mc Koy farm was so successful that school officials and Home Demonstration Agencies came out and used it to demonstrate new farm technologies or how a successful farm should be run.

My mom's family lived in a large 2 story frame home built by slaves. Grandpa devised a plan to make the farm

...for the *Entrepreneur*

productive enough to maintain his family and also to aid him in building a new home. He chose 100 trees and nurtured them over the years. My mom remembers walking around behind him and watching him and choose one tree over another. She wasn't quite sure why he would walk around and 'just look' at the trees. When the trees were ready, he contracted with a company to turn them into lumber thus saving money.

Within little more than 10 years he had built his family a new home. It is now remodeled and enlarged for the family to enjoy. I still get chills when I go in and stand next to the cast iron stove in the living room that I know he installed. The rest of the house is much larger and very modern now with a 3 season porch and all new appliances and extra bedrooms; but the old stove (which still works!) is Grandpa's space. My uncle, the first born, owns the land today and leases it for farming tobacco, corn, and soybeans now. It is still earning money from my grandfather's efforts and is now the family vacation home.

Still More Innovators

There were even more entrepreneurs on my Mom's side.

My great uncle Joe owned what they called a Taxi Stand in the 1940s and 50s: He was an independent Taxi driver. He took business men from Clinton to-and-from the

My Now...

Fayetteville airport right next to the Air Force Base, 30 miles away. Like my grandfather driving people to Ft. Bragg, at that time it was too expensive and inconvenient for most people, especially business men, to travel by bus or taxi just to get to the airport. My grandfather and my great uncle saw a need and they each filled it. They organized and managed their days so that they could accommodate their customer's schedules and became business owners.

My great uncle Bill owned a diner in Harlem New York in the 30s and 40s, right after the Great Depression. He lived there during the Harlem Renaissance. He worked in the finest restaurants and hotels for years until he saved enough money to purchase a diner right across from the World Trade Center. After retiring he moved back to North Carolina and was a part-time caterer.

During the same time, three of my great aunts, Sally, Jeanette and Hattie, Bill's sisters, also moved to Harlem and worked in the Garment District until they saved enough money to buy their own Beauty Shop and a 15-room, 3-story apartment building from their combined savings. I remember visiting the Beauty shop and apartment building when I was very young and my parents tried to get me to understand the significance of their entrepreneur efforts but again I did not understand at that time. Now I see what they were so excited about and once again I wish I was old enough to 'appreciate it' back then.

Conclusion

With segregation and racism more rampant then that it is today, many of my family thrived by owning their own businesses. They did not take no for an answer and did what they needed to do to own businesses and to be entrepreneurs most likely without knowing exactly how significant their efforts were. They organized, managed and they were bold in taking risks. They planned their goals and never lost focus. They were all very successful.

DNA

I never quite understood my determination to not just be complacent but to walk to the beat of another drummer; to think outside of the box and understand my discomfort with working for someone else. I have never been truly happy working in an office and in fact, my favorite job was being a flight attendant. Not because of the perceived glitz and glamour, but because I was not confined somewhere with a supervisor or co-workers constantly with me. It was an element of freedom, flying the friendly skies, meeting all kinds of new people, going all over the place. But still, as fun as it was it still wasn't the complete freedom I craved. As a young adult, I had always wanted to own my own clothing boutique and create my own magazine. I didn't understand where it came from really.

My Now...

I have tried to various Direct Selling companies but I was never a person that enjoyed quotas, deadlines, formulas or rules. Working for private and public companies, I have seen the glass ceiling up close, no matter my efforts, I found others progressing faster and farther than me. By being my own boss allows me to be me and challenge myself and not watch as others succeed over me. I have never been interested in the 'internal' corporate ladder; I always wondered what else was 'out there,' somewhere *out there*.

Now, I finally found my passion; writing, speaking, teaching and coaching. At AFC (Andrea Foy Consulting), I conduct workshops and seminars on topics such as: Women's Issues, Business Skills, Diversity, Image Consulting, Personal Success Strategic Plan and the Hire Power Series. I am a Certified Professional Coach, a Certified Diversity Training Consultant and a Certified Facilitator with Moovin4ward Presentations. I am also an Independent Certified John Maxwell Leadership Coach, Speaker and Teacher.

As a result of thinking about contributing a chapter to this book, I now have found an insight to myself and more respect for my maternal and paternal family and the value and lessons learned from them. I know my ancestors are happy that I am following in their hard-worked entrepreneurial pursuits.

...for the Entrepreneur

It's Our Turn

I know I am probably not the only one with relatives that were so innovative. Chances are you have people in your past who were as innovative as mine were. We need to go back to that mentality again, to see a need and fill it: To have a goal and save money to work for it, to *just do it*. Roll up our sleeves and figure out a way to do it ourselves. We need to not worry about whether we are supposed to it or who is going to stop us and **Just Do It**! Our ancestors **Did It**; more of us need to **Do It**. I believe we can **DO IT**!

References:
http://www.merriam-webster.com/dictionary/entrepreneur
http://dictionary.reference.com/browse/entrepreneur
http://www.thefreedictionary.com/Entrepreneur
http://dictionary.reference.com/browse/enterprise

My Now...

Elisa S. Gary

Elisa, Director of **"The 1st Ministry Initiative"** is a speaker, author, and visionary with a passion for God, people and the restoration of families. She has branded herself as The Inspiration Coach, noting "motivation is external, but inspiration comes from within". She hosts weekly conference calls, during which she delivers powerful lessons; challenging her listeners to push past their current circumstance, make their mess their message, and to be actively engaged in their lives. In 2011, Elisa founded a women's empowerment group called **The Complete Woman Fellowship** (T.C.W.F). Her organization encourages self-development, overcoming obstacles, and mental well-being. Elisa firmly believes suffering in silence, voids your testimony and inhibits personal breakthrough. She is the President of **Inspired Conferences**, a virtual platform, which she uses to deliver conferences that impact, empower, and inspire change. Her new book **"12 Steps to Conquering Your Inner Bully"** can be purchased at www.theinspirationcoach.net

Find out more by visiting www.inspiredconferences.com

...for the Entrepreneur

The Business of You

Elisa Gary

Have you ever heard the phrase, "You're not selling a product, you're selling yourself"? This quote is not an uncommon one among the business world. However, far too many anxious entrepreneurs start businesses, and invest hundreds, sometimes thousands of dollars, before they have bought into their most important product; themselves. Among the many lessons you will learn while reading this book, I want to be sure that personal efficacy; that is, the belief that one can overcome obstacles and achieve goals, is one of them. In addition, I will teach you to perform a personal S.W.O.T analysis, capitalize on your life experience, and above all things enjoy being you!

Buy Into You

Current and aspiring entrepreneurs are usually driven by the idea of being their own boss, pursuing their own ideas, and realizing significant financial rewards. Despite most ventures ending in failure within the first 18 to 26 months of launching, thousands of aspirants embark on the road of

My Now...

entrepreneurship every day. Interestingly enough, these goals seem to closely mimic the three basic rights outlined in the Declaration of Independence, those being; life, liberty, and the pursuit of happiness. Much like life is to American citizens, being your own boss seems to be the fundamental right within the entrepreneurial world, of which all other rights of entrepreneurs are derived. In addition, I would offer, that while "being your own boss" may be your expressed right as an entrepreneur, liberty within the business arena can prove to be an urban myth. The notion that "the customer is always right" can quickly overshadow your individual liberties and leave you with feelings that strongly contrast happiness. More importantly, it is quite easy to lose one's self in the maze of tax law, customer service complaints, marketing strategies, and advertising campaigns.

While some companies, do manage to survive the preliminary phases of the business cycle without clearly revealing the face, or identity of the company; it is far more difficult to persevere the turbulent seas of expansion, and maintaining customer loyalty when this crucial step has not been completed. Many entrepreneurs struggle with defining the face of their business, because they have failed to clearly define themselves. To do this you must have a clear outline of your strengths, recognize areas in which you could improve, be prepared to take advantage of opportunities to grow, and realize that there will always be people who will not be supportive of your goals, or secretly wishing that you'll fail.

...for the Entrepreneur

Amidst these truths, it is essential for you to understand that you are your most valued asset. If you don't believe in yourself, it is next to impossible to run a successful business. More importantly, it is imperative that you are clear on whom you are, what your purpose is, and how you will go about fulfilling it. If you don't invest time to shape your identity, it will be impossible to accurately position yourself within your personal and professional environments.

Conducting A Personal S.W.O.T Analysis

From an entrepreneur's perspective, the reputation of their business is everything. It is crucial for customers to recognize its value, to understand that the business fills a need in a way that others fail to, and as a result, continues to practice brand loyalty. Employees are expected to be honest, work hard to keep the business afloat, and put in overtime when there are critical tasks that must be completed. Entrepreneurs want their competitors to both respect them and to take them seriously. Although competition is supposed to help shape a non-biased market, it's hard to argue that the much more common theme of competitors is to kill out its competition. As individuals, we need the same principles to apply in our personal lives. The only difference is that employees are categorized as family, customers as friends and competitors... well, you could find a few of them in each category previously mentioned, but you

My Now...

may often feel that they are enemies. Let's compare them visually.

	Juxtaposing Professional & Personal Relationships		
Employees	▪ Honesty is Implied ▪ Requires Mutual Investment ▪ Can Require Additional Time Commitment		Family
Customers	▪ Recognize Value ▪ Fill a Need ▪ Expect Loyalty		Friends
Competitors	▪ Need for Respect ▪ Can Create a Hostile Environment		Enemies

You may be asking yourself "What does this have to do with anything?" Once you understand the roles of the people around you, and how they have been or can potentially impact your life, it is easier to position both them and yourself within the boundaries of your life. More importantly, you gain insight into who you are, the dynamic of your relationships, and how to better operate within your personal and professional environments. Once you understand the categories, roles, and positioning of people within your professional and personal environment, you can conduct a more comprehensive and detailed S.W.O.T analysis of your life.

S.W.O.T. is the business acronym for strengths, weaknesses, opportunities, and threats. It is a means for business owners, venture capitalist, and investors to identify

...for the Entrepreneur

the positives and negatives within a company (S-W), and outside the company's external environment (O-T). Although it can be particularly time consuming, skipping this crucial step can result in bankruptcy, with little to no hope of recovery. This concept applied to the context of personal identity, is just as critical to the success of your personal existence.

First you must critique you internal environment, by identifying your strengths and weaknesses.

Strengths

Strengths can be both tangible and non-tangible in nature. These can be things that come naturally, or that you have learned to do. Please understand, that though you may feel what your good at serves no real purpose, you must begin to realize that it is a specific answer to a problem that you have yet to discover. You may find that there are certain things you are consistently praised for, even when you feel it may be unwarranted. For some, its communication, others you give great advice. Are you a social butterfly or a natural networker? Great! Join a networking group, and go often. Looking to shape your career as a professional speaker? Join a local Toastmasters club, and offer to be a speaker. This will help you not only develop new friendships with synergistic people, but to ensure your regular interaction with those that will help shape your talents.

Strengths are not always apparent. They may be things that scare you just at the thought of displaying them. This does not change the fact that it is a strength. You must overcome your fear and step outside of your comfort zone.

Weaknesses

If you are not careful, weaknesses can completely halt your progress. You must determine the origin of the weaknesses and put a plan in motion to address them.

Are you a huge procrastinator? Procrastinators are most often suffering from negative self-talk. It is hard to move forward when you have pre-programmed yourself with thoughts of failure. Your fabricated illustration of your life may appear to be real if it's paired with lack of support and disrespect from your family and/or friends.

Maybe you're issue is that you've been blessed with a broad skill set (i.e. graphics, website design, writing, book keeping), but this makes you less focused, and diverts your time from your goals. You may not have a choice, due to a less than favorable financial situation or a non-existent budget. Just as, it is hard to both manage and brand a business on a limited budget, it can seem next to impossible to pursue your dreams when you can barely make ends meet. Overcome this weakness, by bartering your skills in exchange for services you need. This will free up some time to focus on building your strengths and realizing your goals.

Next, you must focus on your external environment. This includes your opportunities and threats.

Opportunities

You must not wait for an opportunity to arise before you begin to prepare for it. Opportunities are things that lye, for the most part, outside of your control. However, grooming your strengths and tackling your weaknesses will prepare you to take advantage of opportunities and build awareness that will assist in your decision-making, and enables you to act on opportunities in a timely manner. Business opportunities may come in the form of a vacated market sector due to an ineffective competitor, strategic alliances, the emergence of social media, and new social networking or technology. However, in your personal life, it may be a change of heart by family members, a promotion at work, connecting with your children, or earning your degree.

Taking steps to seize an opportunity is not always easy. There will be hurdles to overcome, maybe even newly discovered weaknesses; but know that you will always grow in the process.

Threats

No one needs a lesson in comparing themselves to others. When it comes to personal crucifixion, some of us could win a gold medal. The world around us is filled with external stressors, pitfalls, and unsupportive people. Our own families, which seemingly should be the most fertile environment, conducive to growth and nourishment, most often are dry, malnourished and snake ridden.

We often see threats as something that will ultimately be our demise, a proverbial tornado that will end our personal and/or professional lives as we know it. I would like to offer another option. Remove the stigma of the threat. What is the worst that could come from the situation? Face it dead on! While it's easy to resort to obsessing over future outcomes, this brings little to no resolve. It is better to reevaluate your strengths, and develop a detailed plan.

Conducting a personal S.W.O.T analysis is not an easy feat, but it's not meant to be. It should be an ongoing cycle of personal growth, and external assessment, learning, and goal realization. Don't let your talents go to waste. While it can be daunting, continuing to engage in this process will prove to be both lucrative and beneficial. Be present in your own life. It is easy to read these words, arrive at many epiphanies, yet walk away and do nothing. I urge you to do the exact opposite. Pledge to conquer your inner bully; that is the fear that threatens to strip you of your dreams, and the doubt that paralyzes you on the path to greatness!

...for the Entrepreneur

Part 2: Preparation & Planning

My Now...

Dr. Kreslyn Kelley

Life experienced first, then, academically trained - Educator, Entrepreneur, Trainer, Mentor, Coach, Community Servant and Activist.

Kreslyn left the field of education, to start her own business, Premier Leadership Academy. Her passion is still educating children, but now also includes educating adults. Her platform has moved beyond the school house, to conference rooms, auditoriums, and office space. Her subject matter has changed from reading, writing and arithmetic to leadership, diversity, character building, team building, goal setting, and helping others identify individual purpose and passion. Dr. Kelley's ultimate goal, is always to help anyone seeking higher ground realize that it is not only possible, but it is inevitable! Her simple, yet dynamic, approach is making herself real and transparent to others by sharing her own stories of challenges and triumphs. She is one of the featured authors of the book, *My Vision, My Plan, My NOW!*

For more information, visit her site, **kreslynkelley.com** or **placademy.net**.

...for the *Entrepreneur*

Stop, Drop & Roll
Dr. Kreslyn Kelley

"Lord, you know the plans you have for me, plans to prosper me and not to harm me, to give me hope and a future." I screamed this on the inside of me, with tormenting tears while I sat at the desk of my "day" job, and as I do at least once a month; however, this day was particularly agonizing. I could not lay my hands on why I felt so discontent in that moment, but I found everything in the world to complain and to be unhappy about in my current position, in life, and just in general.

On this day in January 2013, I actually dropped my head and prayed, repeatedly, the Jeremiah 29:11 scripture quoted above. Ironically, I received a phone call immediately afterwards, and the gentleman on the other end said, "I've been praying and I want to offer you a position." The position was completely aligned with my skill set. It paid $25k more than what I make in my current position, plus I have great working relationship with the employer for we serve on a board together. Instantly, I was like, Eureka!! This must be my answer. This phone call could not have happened at a more perfect time; or, so I thought.

Excitingly yet hesitantly, I accepted the offer. I had a few more days to ponder, because the offer had to be presented to and voted on by the organization's board. There was no doubt in my mind that they would unanimously vote in my favor. I had served as a consultant with the newly formed organization, and the board members were well aware, first hand, of my expertise. Furthermore, I discussed this opportunity with my friends and family, and everyone seemed very enthusiastic and wanted to know the details, but as the evening drew near, the exhilaration soon disappeared and anxiety and discontentment kicked in again. It was in those very moments that I realized I made a mistake. I acted purely off emotion, and did not take time to identify why I was feeling discontent.

Finally, I realized that my unrest was not due to a desire for more money and/or different position. I was uneasy because I was neglecting the work of my own business for my day job and many other things. I was not balanced. I was not meeting my goals. I was not focused. Therefore, I was discontent because I was not living out my dreams. I did not feel purposeful or relevant.

Hence, I was forced to make the dreaded phone call to inform my professional friend that I must renege on my acceptance. I was very sorry, because I knew how much he and others wanted me to assume that position. However, I explained to him that if I took that position, it would not be long before I would feel the same way I was feeling the day he called me and offered it. Then, he found some comfort in his understanding of my rational. We both thought it was "the" answer to all of our problems in that very moment; but, the truth was that this "new" organization, which has a lofty purpose for existing, deserved to have a director who could give 150% of their time and energy. And, I did not have that to give, while trying to run my own business.

My current position provided me the flexibility I needed to do both. I had chosen to go above and beyond what was expected of me in the position, which is considered a good work ethic by most; but, it resulted in the neglect of my own business, and herein laid my problem. I was unfulfilled because I was not balancing my dreams with my other everyday chores and duties. And, had I learned to **STOP** – In the middle of my madness, just hit the brakes and breath, and then, plan time throughout the week to cease from work, **DROP** -dismiss everything, and I do mean everything, so that in my solitude, I can evaluate where I am with all that is expected of me by me and others, and **ROLL** - focus on my dreams, create a plan, modify existing plans, and put the ball back in motion, I could have saved myself and others so much anguish.

My Now...

If the simple technique (STOP, DROP, &ROLL), can be used to save a life during a vicious house fire, imagine the benefit if used figuratively in our personal and professional lives when we feel we are on fire. Let's consider the purpose of this technique, which is taught to thousands of children throughout the year.

STOP – First, the fire victim must be still in order to keep from fanning the flames and hinder those working to quench the fire.

- When we feel like we are on fire, doing nothing is best in order to keep from making things worse for ourselves and others.
- There may be others who can and want to help us, but when we are moving on our own during those times of distress and anxiety, we can miss excellent opportunities for improvement in our business and our sanity.
- Moving around when stressed only adds more tension. Rest is a necessary component for success in our businesses, health, and family lives.

DROP – Next, the fire victim must drop to the ground, getting as low as they can and lying down if possible, while using their hands to cover their face while avoiding facial injuries if at all possible.

...for the Entrepreneur

- Dropping everything, when extremely stressed and irritated, can help one "Save Face." When working through extreme stress, we are more likely to make more mistakes and make decisions that are not well thought out.
- For entrepreneurs, who seek spiritual guidance for their affairs, like I do, physically getting low with our bodies brings us to a place of humility, where we are able pray, upward, or go inward for answers from the highest and innermost places.
- Covering the face is also a good way to block out distractions, which divert us from our dreams and visions. Often we lose sight because of everything else that is going on around us. We must stay focused by closing our eyes and intentionally envisioning what it is we really want.

ROLL - Finally, the fire victim rolls on the ground in an attempt to divest the fire of oxygen, helping to extinguish the flames.

- There is no rolling before the victim stops and drops. So once we have taken the time to cease and pull ourselves together, analyze the situation, pray, and/or go inward, remember our dreams, then we have permission to move again.

- This movement can smother the oxygen, the very life of the fire, as we realign with our new stance and focus.
- Movement with a purpose can save our lives, and can save the existence of our small businesses, even when we have to work a day job.

It is not easy working for yourself while also working for others. However, if the entrepreneurial dream is inside of you, then it is necessary that you investigate it and give it a fair shot. Often, we become anxious because the vision is clear and exciting. We think it will happen tomorrow. Of course, there are times when people, ideas, and dreams literally become overnight successes. However, more often than not, they take years. Consequently, people give up on them when they don't manifest in a flash.

For you, the entrepreneur, who has to work in order to support your family and your dream, do not allow yourself to be overwhelmed and engulfed in a flame of discouragement, because you are not content with your current job, position, and/or pay. Just stay focused on your dreams. The discontentment has a purpose. It is there to remind you that you have a dream. So, do not become frustrated and to give up. Instead, in those moments of the greatest distress, simply STOP, DROP, and ROLL. Then, if you want to take it to another level, do it before the frustrations

...for the Entrepreneur

arise. You'll be amazed at yourself. You are capable of doing it all. Just do it right and do it NOW!

My Now...

Mark W. Wiggins

Mark "The Speaker Man" Wiggins, an International speaker, trainer, author and entrepreneur is the CEO of Xtreme Effort Speaking. He has held leadership and management positions within several national retail companies, such as Foot Locker, Eddie Bauer, and Levi Strauss & Co. He has trained corporate, community, and association leaders in the Washington, DC area on the topics of customers, leadership and human performance.

He is the author of *Permission to Succeed: the Only Person Who Needs to Give it is You*; *MTXE the Formula for Success*; and more. He is also one of the featured authors of the book, *My Vision, My Plan, My NOW!*

Get my information right now! Text Speakerman to 90210.

...for the Entrepreneur

When a Deck is Not a Deck

Mark Wiggins

Think about your dreams. Yes, those dreams you had of becoming a successful entrepreneur. Now, when you think about those dreams and ambitions, does it make you laugh or cry? Most people only get to dream big while they sleep and live out those dreams in their mind. Few dare take the step to the next level. Few ever put into action or dare make the sacrifices to have what they truly want in their life. In truth, your first business and the one that everyone has to face, is the business of YOU. You have to focus on your dreams, your vision, your passion and then create a plan and NEVER give up until you achieve it.

Let's face it, entrepreneurism is a disease! My father's side of the family has this running joke that you are not a true Wiggins until you had your own business... in fact several of them. I grew up believing this was true. As a matter of fact my father had many business ventures. He was ahead of his time on many of them, but he was an entrepreneur determined to be successful. My first memory of my father's business venture is the decision to buy a laundry mat in the

My Now...

inner city of Cleveland, Ohio. It was a great time. I remember the nights counting cold hard cash and rolling them up and taking them to the bank. Not only did my father have a laundry mat, he also had a dry cleaners attached to the Laundry mat. Who does that? Well that was back in the late 70's and early 80's. But, my father wasn't the only one in the family with a business; my Uncle James also had many businesses. My favorite was the Shaw- St. Clair Skating Rink. I grew up at the skating rink with my other cousins. We would skate all night, but we had to work all day. Uncle James' wife Lois was also an entrepreneur. She had a daycare which was located inside the Shaw-St. Clair skating ring. What an awesome way to make use of that space during the day. The funny thing is that my aunt Lois made such an impact on her family that two of her daughters have their own successful day cares today and one of James' sons has also stared a daycare. My cousin, April, received some great advice from her mother, Lois, before she passed away, she told April to move to Maple Heights to be near Uncle Mckliney, my dad, so he could help her with her business. She did just that, and I am sure she's glad she did.

My mother, on the other hand, led me to believe that my dad and his family were crazy for trying all these businesses. She said that her side of the family was the sane side. That was until I found out my mom's brother, Marion, was a successful entrepreneur on his own right. He too has had many business ventures. On a recent trip to visit my uncle in

Portland Oregon, I discovered that he had similar experiences to me that I tried as an adult. However, his most successful business is his tennis club, in Portland, Oregon. An African-American owning a business in Portland Oregon? Who does that? He did. Now, since my father has passed, we speak often. I have also found out that he actually owned a traveling semi-pro industrial league basketball team. Talk about an entrepreneurial disease, he has it bad. I don't have enough space to tell you all the other things he has done. Even his sons have it bad as well. The oldest son, Anthony, is a teaching tennis pro, and works at the club. The youngest, Ramon, has a clothing line in New York. All that back ground and I wonder why I am an entrepreneur. What great inspiration.

I was indoctrinated as a kid to believe that jobs were safe to have, but you needed to have your own thing on the side, your "side hustle", if you were ever going to truly be happy. However, that was small thinking.

When you play at something you get kid results, when you have passion hunger and drive, you create something and grow it. My father told me that he never really shared his visions about greatness with too many people. He said that when you share your vision with people they get jealous or try their best to bring you down or talk you out of what you want to do. But he shared a secret with me, he told me something that I held on to, and now use when I speak to people who have dreams. He told me that

"My dreams are just as stupid as yours."

I was offended when he said that. I was tricked, he just told me not share my dreams, and then I did, and he tells me my dreams are stupid. That was one of those parent Jedi mind tricks. What he was teaching me? That everyone has a dream, and to other people those dreams sound stupid, I'm sorry to say, but it's true. If we both share dreams right now, we would find out that we both have these crazy wild dreams and on the surface they do sound stupid. But they are YOUR dreams, so it does not matter what people think. So, the next time you share your dreams, and somebody says, "Man that sounds stupid," just reply with "well what are your dreams?" Enough said.

When I was in high school, my dad started flipping houses. He was doing this before it was the "thing" to do. I hated working on the houses. They were dirty, in the hood, and I didn't get to rest on Saturdays like my friends did. Most every Saturday morning, bright and early, the clock would ring and he would call up stairs. I would grudgingly roll out of bed and meet the smell of pancakes, sausages, eggs, hash browns, juice and fruit. There's nothing like a big home cooked breakfast on Saturday morning. Sure helped changed things a bit for me.

...for the Entrepreneur

He took me to this house on E 93rd in Cleveland Ohio. It was the first house he had purchased and needed to fix it up to rent it.

"We're going to do a project together. We're going to build a deck on this house."

Somehow I was not as excited as he was. I saw a beat up, rickety, leaning, death trap of a deck. If you stepped on it the wrong way you would die. He hands me a hammer, and says to tear it down. With a big smile, I looked at him and in my mind said now you are talking. I began to rip, pull, and throw. But the more I worked and the harder I worked, the less I seemed to be getting done. My dad comes to check on me about 2 hours after we get there and wants to know if I'm done.

What the... Done??? NO!

In reality I had not made much progress. So, he left me again told me to keep working and to figure it out.

My dad was good about that, he would teach people by putting them in situations and then coach them through to the solution. Being determined I went back to it and continued to tear up stuff. Another 2 hours went by and my dad came back. Progress had been made; however, I still was a long way from completing the task. "Let's go eat," he said. Besides, "let's go home," those were my favorite 3

My Now...

words. We jumped into the station wagon and went to one of his favorite dives for food. He asks,

"How do you see your deck in your mind when it is finished?"

"What?"

I didn't see anything and I hoped they never opened the back door.

"No, I cannot see that. All I can see is the problem in front of me and the task at hand. I cannot see how this deck will add any value to the house or the purpose of even having a deck. Why did you pick this house anyway?"

"I have a question for you: Are diamonds always pretty and shinny?"

"Of course"

"No, they are not. As matter of fact the process to mine diamonds is a very hard and dangerous process. Diamonds are one of the toughest materials in the world, they are covered by coal and made under pressure. You have to work and work to get to the diamond and then spend time cutting away the parts you don't want to get the look and shine you want. One of the things that make them so valuable is not what you see; it's what was cut away and what's left. Think about the gemologist that cuts the

...for the *Entrepreneur*

diamond. He has to already have a plan before he starts cutting away the diamond, because once its cut, it's gone. So, it's best to have a vision of what you want before you finish so you won't throw away, or cut away something you may need later."

So we continued to eat and my father said the dreaded:

"Back to work!"

I went back to the deck with a different approach this time. I looked at it like I had already torn it down, and looked at was what was left, and decided that not all of the structure needed to come down. I looked at it differently. Then I began to see what the deck would look like when it was done. I ran and got my father and said, "Dad, I think I see what I want to do with this deck." I explained to him what I wanted and pointed to the spaces and rails that would go there. Did I mention that I have never ever built a deck before in my life, nor was I handy with the tools, much to the disappointment of my father. He said, "You have learned a very important lesson. In order to be a good business man or great one, you have to see the things that people don't see; you have to see the end before you start; and you have to have a plan. Once you have that, you can fill in the pieces and achieve whatever you want."

**Finding the Diamond is the easy part;
Knowing what to do with it is the hardest part –**

My Now...

that takes vision and creativity.

After that lesson, the deck was down and ready to make a new one. I looked at my dad with the face of young confused child as to say what's next? He handed me a shovel and said, DIG. WHAT? I had this great idea for a deck and he said, "DIG." But this time before we started digging, I asked where?

"That's a better question," he said. He marked off the places where he wanted us to dig, and we went to work. Each hole had to be the same depth. It appeared that we were taking more care and planning to place these holes than I did in tearing down the deck. Once the holes were dug, we poured the cement and set the standards. Afterwards, we leveled them off, braced them, and checked the levels again before we left. My favorite words finally came,

"Let's go home."

I asked my father why we spent so much time and care on the standards, holes, etc. it didn't seem to make sense to me. I really couldn't wait to see what would happen, I could hardly sleep. We got to the house the next morning and I ran to the back to see what happened. The poles were set and seemed to be straight. I looked at my dad,

...for the *Entrepreneur*

"If this next part is not done correctly, you will have to start it over."

I got nervous because I didn't want to make a mistake. I didn't want to start over and I didn't want to do anything to mess up my progress. Sensing that something was wrong, my father asked me,

"What's up? You seem hesitant today."

"I am scared to make a mistake so the best thing for me to do is to sit back and watch."

"What's the worst thing that could happen?"

"We would have to start over."

"Right, but that's not ALL bad, it could actually be a good thing, gaining knowledge is the bases for growth."

My father went on to tell me that in building things much like business, you will always have to redo things, start over or make modifications. The key to success is to be knowledgeable about what you are doing, take your time and build your base knowledge, and then proceed with caution; not fear, but caution.

The difference between being fearful and being cautious is that when you are cautious you are careful, you can catch things before they get out of hand or if need be scrap the whole project because it will not work. Fear will paralyze you, and you will not do anything and opportunities will quickly disappear and go to the person who is better prepared.

> **"You fail, if you don't learn something during the process, and refuse to learn something about the process"**
>
> The Speaker Man

We continued to put the wood down and nail the pieces into place. Once we got the first floor down the other two levels seem to fall in place. I improved with each hit of the hammer as my father gave me immediate feedback on proper technique. The more I hit, the better I became. It took less and less effort. Before I knew it, the feeling of accomplishment was starting to build. For the most part, the deck I had envisioned the day before came to life. There were some minor adjustments, there were some do-overs, and there were some boards thrown away. Although they didn't fit the original plan, they were modified and used as handrails, steps and accents for the deck.

When the deck was finished, we went inside climbed to the top level on the second floor. My father opened the door and said,

"Go ahead take the first step."

...for the Entrepreneur

"WHAT? Are you nuts? I'm not doing that!"

"Why not? What's the worst that could happen?"

"I could die. That's the worst that could happen,"

With a smile on his face he responded, "Yes son, you are correct. That would be the worst thing that could happen, but go ahead." The lesson learned that day was simply this you have to have faith in your work. You have to believe that you have taken the time to lay a solid foundation. As an entrepreneur you need to proceed with caution and information not fear? Changes and adjustment will be necessary. But above all you must have a vision and a plan of what you want before you start.

My dad started talking to me about how I should have confidence my ability and work to take the first step. He wanted me to now that if I don't take the first step, I will never know if the deck is safe and sturdy. He then asked me question: "Do you know how the eagle learns how to fly? It flaps its wings and flies. And how does it know to flap its wings? I don't know... The mother eagle just pushes it out of the nest." With that, he pushed me out the door to take the first step on something that I help build. My dad was strange like that.

My dad sat me down and proceeded to share with me the following crumbs of wisdom that I now share with you:

My Now...

Son, I have learned that no matter how many times I want to try something or do a new business there comes a time where you either do, or you don't. If you don't think you can, you are right, and if you think you can you are also right. You have to trust yourself, trust in your ability, know your limitations, and get help and guidance when you need it. The sign of a good business man is not that he can build business, or create something from nothing, but rather it's that he trusts himself completely to do the job and do it well. Because if you don't believe and trust in yourself, how will anyone else have the confidence to take a chance on you? Let me answer, they won't.

We still had more work to do that day, but I got a double surprise. My dad said my favorite two phrases at the same time:

"Let's go eat," and "Let's go home."

So, let's wrap this up. If you really want to have a business or start that venture and get off the bench as an entrepreneur here are 5 things you need remember:

1) Don't be afraid to see things that are not there
2) Get the knowledge and mentorship you need to make great business decisions
3) Take time to build a strong foundation
4) Have a vision and create the plan
5) Take action

...for the Entrepreneur

A dream will remain a dream, until you take action and get off the bench and into the starting line-up of life.

My Now...

Nysheva-Starr

Nysheva-Starr is an innovator, writer, designer, speaker, and performing artist. She is the CEO of I-Gaian, Inc, a company primarily aimed at fostering cumulative growth for African Americans. She is the founder, creator, and arranger of Safari Kwenye Nafsi: Journey to Self, the African American Right to Rites of Passage Experience, a comprehensive and progressive series of passages geared towards documenting age set journeys for Black Americans. She has written a series of books which will be published soon, highlighting the principles that make early development successful, especially as it relates to Blacks. As an innovator/designer, she recently patented a garment she made for yoga practitioners. She is also one of the featured authors of the book, *My Vision, My Plan, My NOW!*

Follow her on twitter at **@nyshevastarr**. For more information on the passages, send an email to **info@i-gaianinc.com** and/or visit the website at **www.i-gaiainc.com**.

...for the Entrepreneur

Prerequisites to Entrepreneurial You

Nysheva-Starr

So, you wanna be an entrepreneur, huh? Why? Because you want to make more money. Because you want to be your own boss. Or because you have a really great idea. Well, guess what? So what! The truth is: Everyone cannot be an entrepreneur. Anyone is not fit for the job. And this is regardless of how much you might really want to be one and regardless of how big the lure is from society showcasing entrepreneurship as 'the be all and end all' answer to your success. Entrepreneurship is a calling. It is its own *'right to passage.'* One has to 'be with' the architectonics to be granted the *right* to pass through the 'world of self developed ingenuity.' Assessing whether you are called to become an entrepreneur can save you time, money and resources, including granting you more time, money and resources to allocate towards that which you *are* called to do. So, how do you determine whether entrepreneurship *is* for you? You Evaluate first. You Reflect second. And *how* do you do that?

My Now...

To determine your potential for success as an entrepreneur, you should explore your temperament, ethic and resilience as it relates to seven principles. There is somewhat of a ranking with the principles whereas, the sooner it is listed; the more crucial you should consider it in choosing entrepreneurship or not. Below are the seven principles with accommodating questions that highlight the principle's essence.

The Seven S's to Sole Success or S4

1) <u>Surety</u>: 'Is Entrepreneurship for Me?'
2) <u>Stringency</u>: 'Does my Vision have Precision?'
3) <u>Study</u>: 'What Do I Need to Learn?'
4) <u>Scribe</u>: 'How Can I Measure my Progress?'
5) <u>Sacrifice</u>: 'Am I Committed?'
6) <u>Standard</u>: 'Can I Separate Personal(ism) from Professionalism?'
7) <u>Support</u>: 'Who is Keeping me Galvanized?'

How sure are you of your desire for entrepreneurship? The 'principle of surety' says: 'Ask yourself about the certainty of your desire?' Specifically, what are your reasons? What guides those reasons? Is there a hierarchy with your reasoning? Like, is fortune measured the same as freedom and/or fame? Let's explore. Entrepreneurship requires two main things: time and money...or is it money and time?!. Doesn't matter. They're in the same category. And either

...for the Entrepreneur

more of one can be successfully leveraged over to the other, making it whereas the other is no longer deficient, if indeed it was deficient to begin with. Back to the issue. If your pinnacle reason for wanting to be an entrepreneur is because you want to make a lot more money, but, you ain't got no 'real' money to begin with; then, not only are you going to be broke, but, you're also going to be miserable because you don't have any time to make more money or any extra money to invest more time. Besides, opening a business in an area that solely or mostly has the potential to accumulate wealth **can** quite possibly mean wealth, but, it **will** lack the ability to accumulate longer longevity. Being impassioned about what you're doing ensures that you can do it for a long time. Interestingly enough, if freedom and fame are your premier high points of entrepreneurship, you'd be glad to know that, although the aforementioned two 'reasons' does not mean that you will become rich, at least with the formative 'reason' of wanting fortune, there is an encasement of freedom and fame. Otherwise, if freedom leads your 'surety' factor in your quest for entrepreneurship; then you can be successful opening a business making the same money you were making when you were employed by someone else, but, your added autonomy allows you to value that role more. If fame leads your 'surety' factor in your quest for entrepreneurship; then you would have to be known for something that makes you superior and/or favorably different from others in the same field, whereas

My Now...

others' demand for your exceptional service is a constant they are not willing to part with.

Entrepreneurship requires specificity. This is one of the reasons why business plans are suggested - to visualize what is theoretical - to see with the eyes what, in thought, is only seen with the mind. In order to exhaust one's specificity, a niche has to be carved out. Your niche, in business, is your special blueprint to success. A person's niche can be discovered through the 'principle of stringency.' Stringency is the process by which one is very selective in the choosing and manifestation of their niche. In other words, it is the way in which one crafts a concept, making it particular to his/her strengths plus strategic precision with planning how that niche will materialize. When selecting something to be an entrepreneur in, you want to choose something that 'speaks to you' so that you can go on and 'speak to others about it.' Stringency has the ability to add to success because its simplicity doesn't allow for much deviation. Maximizing on a stringent concept happens much easier than if the concept were not stringent. So, though niche finding may take a while, it *is* worth it. How do you set out to find your niche? Well, let's see. Since your niche will probably be connected to the things that you are naturally strong at, you might want to start there. Like, if you're an extroverted communicator who enjoys helping people in a personal way, maybe your niche revolves around being a coach, speaker or consultant. If you feel that you have an intricate, strategic side that you'd

...for the Entrepreneur

like to leverage, perhaps your niche can be formed around designing and implementing efficacious and optimal organization tools for businesses. What if you believe that your niche is centered on/around incorporating your love for the arts; perhaps you'd be interested in opening a business as an arts liaison where you offer people the chance to experience any art mediums that appeals to them - just for fun. Who wouldn't want to be a graphic designer for a day? Or an actor? Or a photographer? The point is - be stringent about what your inclination within yourself leans towards to increase the destination outside of yourself that you're aiming for.

Now, this third principle in one's quest for entrepreneurship is often overlooked because aspirants tend to rely on the beliefs that 1) 'I can learn as I go;' 2) someone *else* is gonna *tell* me; or 3) someone *else* is gonna *teach* me. Now, even though all of those beliefs *may* be true, it is also possibly true, that they will happen...*eventually*. So, why wait until the moment arrives to 'get ready' for something that is eventual anyway, when you can 'be prepared' for it *before* it arrives? Not studying ahead of time is one of the most misguided perceptions about starting your own business. (It's like going to a job interview for a company without having researched the company first). 'Studying' before you venture out can increase how successful you fare with your business, from the onset. And it's not only important and advantageous to learn about entrepreneurship in general, but, also about your particular branch of entrepreneurship. Why? Because it allows you, as the ingénue, to take into consideration four factors: a) is there a physical and/or social 'need' for your product? b) is there a 'want' for your product? c) who is the target market(s) and what sort of pitches work with varying markets? d) what is the economic value of your product (what is the monetary value of the product, taking into consideration its: usefulness, accessibility and necessity against its potential for consistent revenue)?' Now, let's say that your 'product' is an original one and/or a product that may take a while before people catch on to it, well then, it is going to be the 'principle of study' that frames the perceptibility of your product *just* based on how you present your product. 'Study' is the imperative marker that can shape a business plan and/or business proposal that's worth reckoning with. It can put you in the best position to deal with the many facets of owning a business by showcasing realistic examples of what to expect. In this regard, you can develop business savviness even before you've acquired business skillfulness. And who wouldn't want *that* edge. But, remember how you *got ahead* of the game determines how you *stay_ahead* in the game. So, yes, study 'can lead you to it,' but, it can also 'keep you with it.'

Interestingly enough, the fourth principle's worth is constantly an emerging necessity even though we've known its value since we were introduced to it millenniums ago.

...for the Entrepreneur

Writing. I'm not referring to free writing that's aimed at 'getting the juices' flowing, although that's cool. I'm referring to writing down the 'juice that's already flown ' - your business ideas. And this can be anything, well, actually, it should be everything - from ambience if its a location business to online marketing if its not. (This is separate from having a business plan insofar as it is in 'notations' and 'list' form as oppose to in-depth explanations & chronologic). Writing stuff down serves a two-fold purpose. In the first instance, you can centralize your desires for your business, without risking forgetting something that you believe is crucial. In the second instance, writing holds you accountable. It silently persuades you to be productive. How? In order to be sure that productivity is aggregating, the daily 'to do' list should be regarded as an essential 'must have' (& must do). Its benefit heightens '**when it is written down to be scorned upon'** throughout your day. In other words, the 'to do' list becomes the 'little black book' of importance. With that said, it is imperative not to confuse writing something down with typing it into a device. The latter absently employs the hands portion of the body being non-absently directed by the mind portion of the brain whereas the former consciously employs the whole body, mind and spirit since it is normal to form a visceral connection to 1) experiencing yourself writing something down and 2) seeing *your* written down words in front of you. Even more exciting is the idea of accomplishment which comes from having done something on the list. When that happens,

My Now...

embellish in crossing *that thing* done, out. This action is a silent, yet active motivator to your self's diligence as the day progresses. Never take for granted having done something each day as you move towards your vision of entrepreneurship. And again, writing stuff down is a tool that can (& should) be extended into your success once your business is in effect too.

The fifth principle - sacrifice. It's not uncommon for most people to know how important sacrifice is, as most to all people have relationships which require sacrifice. What's commonly unknown is the aspect of sacrifice that lends itself to discipline. Discipline is the ability to stay physically and mentally committed to something even and especially when, emotionally, you want to pull away. Almost any entrepreneur will tell you that their success required hard work. What they simply and not so simply mean is that it required lots more time and money than pre-launching. The rules of thumb are: a) you should invest the same amount of time into your business as you invest in someone else's business. This means that if you're working a full time job, you should expect, while working on your business, to add an additional 40 hours a week and b) you should aim to increase the disposable income amount going towards your business each time you are paid for laboring. Now, *if* you are someone who has other responsibilities too, like, you're a student or a parent and/or spouse; it can be significantly difficult to 'keep up' with your business dreams. It becomes a serious juggling act

...for the Entrepreneur

to get it all in. But, ultimately, if you're serious about being your own boss, you have to 'act as if' you're your own boss way before you're actually acting in the boss role. Discipline is key. Try to do something for your business each day. No feat is too small. And let's be clear, being sacrificial will not give you more time nor will it give you more money for a long time, since, for most start-ups, streamed revenue doesn't happen for a while, yet; it will give you a precise gauge of the level of your tenacity. Knowing where your tenaciousness lies will tell you how sacrificial you should be to reach the goal you're reaching for. If you discover that you are not very tenacious; then, you might want to employ your time differently, like optimizing off of commute times, wait periods or restructuring leisure and/or doing more social activities that are low to no budget to add even more to your business savings lot. If you discover that you are very tenacious, then your consistent regiment of being disciplined with your time and money investments will, more easefully, lead you to your 'soon-to-be-business.'

The sixth principle addresses your approach to your business - operating your business should follow a certain standard. A standard is the external principles that you'll implement to garner consistency, clarity and continuity with and between yourself and others. And this standard should be in place, from the onset, to give you the highest chances of experiencing the least amount of confusion. Creating a

My Now...

business standard can be done from a perspective I call 'the Business Squared' Outlook. The 'Business Squared' outlook is the way in which one looks at entrepreneurship as 'a business' and as 'business.' These two things may seem like the same thing, but, they are not. Looking at entrepreneurship as 'a business' means that the budding entrepreneur approaches situations from the standpoint of being in a 'business mindset' as it relates to his/her own self. Looking at entrepreneurship as 'business' means that the budding entrepreneur approaches situations from the standpoint of 'being in a business mindset' when dealing with others. This is especially beneficial and pertinent when dealing with the varied relationships in our lives. For example, if you're using your personal cell phone for business and your outgoing message to callers is more personal than professional, that may be a turn off. Why? 'Cause it's 'a business' that you're aiming to build and you want to been seen most favorably. If you're introducing a friend to a new concept that hasn't been protected yet, (or even if it is protected), having that friend sign a 'Do Not Compete' Agreement is not a farfetched thing to request. Why? 'Cause its 'business!' Now, what if you're meeting a potential vendor and you're unorganized or too lackadaisical during your initial encounter, that person may not take you too seriously. So be polite, but, be stern, 'cause again, its 'a business' that you're representing. Or, let's say, you have an innovative idea and you decide to tell your parents about it right before you ask

...for the Entrepreneur

them for a loan - yes, your parents should sign a 'Non-Disclosure' form too, but, also a contract should be drawn up to solidify the terms of the loan and both you and them should sign *that*. And in case, you're still wondering why that's necessary...ding, ding, ding, that's right - It's 'Business!' So, Be Professional, Not Personal.

The final principle is the only principle where you, as the budding entrepreneur, do not have to directly *do* anything. Instead, you have to indirectly create a network of people, places and particulars that will support your growth. Support is the main thing, from a business perspective, that can protect you from wanting to quit. By having a growth network made up of people that provoke, places that invoke, and particulars that evoke, you put yourself in the best position to build resistance for the times when a) there is wonderment associated with constantly asking yourself 'why am I doing this?' b) you realize the input-output ratio c) you reminisce of how much easier things were before all the added responsibility d) you just don't want to and/or can't push yourself anymore. Support can come in the form of affirmations, 1 on 1 talks, reflective moments, mantras, inspiration seminars & workshops, daily acknowledgments, quotes, social gatherings and/or business trainings. Virtually anything that has the potential to buffer 'giving up' is support and can be added to your growth network file. Keep in mind that, in order for support to incur growth, it need not be frivolous. Its essential nature is that it benefits the person. It is a communing action that should not be taken for granted because it keeps an individual motivated by being a constant connection to 'getting more' and 'getting better.' If you're not sure how to build your growth network, you can begin with whom and what's already available to and for you. For example, if your mate is a staple in your success, lean over towards that person to receive praise for your new dreams. If your kids keep you on 'Cloud 9' because they believe you are a 'Super Parent,' then, start your dream, using their belief in you. Ultimately, your vision will remain ignited when there is a constant stream of positive thoughts. Those thoughts become constant streamed energy. So, do whatever it takes to stay galvanized!!

Don't let 'the lust' for entrepreneurship distract you from the lessons in it. Don't let 'the look' of entrepreneurship gain more power than the facets of it. And don't let 'the limits' to entrepreneurship form a nebulae of fear from it. By being truthful to yourself as to your avidity (you **want** to move forward), ability (you **know how** to move forward), and availability (you **can** move forward); your actual capacity for moving forward heightens and puts you in the best situation to hold the highest position.

...for the *Entrepreneur*

My Now...

Ava Longfield

Ava has a bachelor's degree from Bowling Green State University, and a master's degree from Kent State University. She previously worked in social work and vocational rehabilitation before becoming an entrepreneur. Over the years, Ava and her family have been involved in various successful business ventures. In 1996, Ava realized her teenage dream and opened a shop in Kent, Ohio. In 2003, Ava and her husband started a property management company in Orlando, Florida. After growing their business and doubling its size, they successfully negotiated the sale of the business to a new team. Ava now calls Atlanta, Georgia, her home, where she operates an upscale home decor and furniture consignment shop. At the end of 2012, the business moved to a new building, doubling the size of the original location. When not engaging with her store customers, Ava is a rock concert aficionado who enjoys traveling and working on home improvement projects.

avalongfield@gmail.com

...for the *Entrepreneur*

Making Lemons into Lemon Margaritas

Ava Longfield

<u>Surviving Corporate Layoffs,
Diving into a New Opportunity & Thriving</u>

Winters can be long and brutal in northeastern Ohio, where I grew up. One February more than a decade ago, a childhood friend died. A few days after her funeral, a huge snowfall blanketed the Cleveland area. At the time, I was running my own store, a fun and funky consignment shop in a college town. As I shoveled a foot of snow to clear the front sidewalk, I suddenly stopped and noticed the peacefulness of the city.

No cars were driving on the roads. No students were walking around. I was by myself. I remember looking up at the perpetually overcast gray sky as tears rolled down my face. I kept thinking about my friend. Then I thought to myself, "If I knew that I was going to pass away tomorrow, what regrets would I have?" Staying in a relationship with the wrong person way too long? Yeah. Choosing a better party school for college? Perhaps. Not working the family business?

My Now...

Maybe. I kept going back to one dream: living in a warmer climate.

I come from a family of small business owners. My father, after holding multiple jobs in the years before I was born, started a business after buying a few truck caps, which led to buying more after the first batch sold. Over the years his business evolved into two retail shops, a van-seat distribution center, a service garage, and an award-winning body of customization work. If that wasn't enough to do, during the middle part of his career, he also bought a tavern in our hometown and transformed it into a popular hangout for local patrons and families. He had certainly found his niche. My extended family has also found success in a variety of industries. So when I decided to foray into a retail business of my own in 1996, it came as no great surprise to most people who knew my family background.

It was a surprise to my family and friends years later, however, when I decided to fly south to the milder temperatures of central North Carolina. Even though my retail shop had been one of the great loves of my life (I truly looked forward to going to work every day), I needed to take this giant step. I knew that if I didn't like living in the South, I could always return home. But I had to find out. There were a few open windows in my life at the time that could have closed at any moment, making me less apt to leave Ohio.

...for the *Entrepreneur*

My three-year business lease was coming up for renewal (Life Window #1). Also, I had recently ended a relationship and taken a break from dating (Life Window #2). Lastly, a good friend of mine who I had known since kindergarten encouraged me to check out the Raleigh/Durham area, and offered me his place as a temporary residence, i.e. cheap boarding (Life Window #3).

I had passed through North Carolina more than once over the years. When I was a young girl, my family would travel to Naples, Florida, annually to visit my grandmother. My dad often enjoyed taking different routes, many times off the beaten path. As we would pass through the small towns and mid-sized cities, I recall looking out of our van window and wondering what it would be like to live there. I saw a man crossing the street in Winston-Salem and wondered what his family and work life entailed. How different was his life from us northern folks who endure over six months of minimal sunshine and boatloads of snow on a regular basis?

As I shoveled snow that cold February day, my face grew wet with tears. I was tired and cold. I walked back into my shop. I had a plan. I was going to go for it and move south. I would either sell my shop or liquidate it, since most of the inventory was mine. (Someday I would like to write a book about the shop. Every day was an adventure!) Moving south would prove to be one of the most pivotal decisions I have ever made.

My Now...

After nine months of planning (and taking some time out to travel throughout Europe with my mother and an Austrian friend), I hit the road to North Carolina. Ten months later in 2000, I met my future husband, Michael, at a charity bachelor auction. A friend had learned about the event, and we decided to check it out before heading out to the area clubs that night. Michael's co-worker had asked him, along with two other colleagues, to be a volunteer bachelor for this cancer center benefit event sponsored by the Raleigh Jaycees. His co-worker's husband had passed away a few years earlier from cancer and she had taken up this cause.

I didn't bid on Michael that night (the date packages with all of the men went for hundreds of dollars up to three thousand dollars). However, Michael and I exchanged business cards that night and agreed to a casual lunch sometime. (It wasn't going to be a date, really.) Two weeks later after our schedules allowed, I offered to pay for our lunch at a Mexican restaurant. I like to think my "bid" for him was pretty darn economical, for twenty-seven bucks. We hit it off, and got engaged a year later. My head was in the clouds, and I felt nothing but good times were ahead! However, life had something else in store for us.

The Raleigh/Durham area had been hit hard by the Dot-Com Bubble. Tech companies were laying off people left and right, and my husband's firm decided to shut down its Research Triangle Park (RTP) facility, which employed about

...for the Entrepreneur

200 people, most of them software engineers. Michael, a Canadian from Ottawa, had accepted a software position at the North Carolina office back in 1996 and transferred shortly thereafter, eventually working his way up to a senior manager position.

In the beginning, we were sure his layoff would be temporary and he would secure full-time employment in no time. Thankfully, during our engagement and throughout my hubby's first year of being laid off, I was still employed. We also had a rainy-day fund set aside. In addition, he received a nice severance package after 18 years of service with the company, and it provided a little bit of a cushion of time for him to find employment. But we also knew the existing finances were finite, and we felt pressure to conserve as much as we could.

We enjoyed ourselves at our October 2002 wedding. A month later, surprise! The small ISP that employed me at the time had to cut staff. As I drove home that last day of work, I secretly hoped this second layoff would be the motivation we needed to finally "get off the bench" and seek out new opportunities. It brought us some order and control over our lives, something which we felt had started dwindling away. We were now ready to select our fate instead of waiting around for some human resources department to decide on a "good enough" resume match for a possible interview.

My Now...

I had been thinking for a few months before my layoff that perhaps we needed to create an opportunity for Michael instead of merely searching for one. Michael had all of these great skills, and if no one else was going to use them, we needed to employ them in some fashion. I had spoken with him about possibly starting or taking over a business. Early on, we had discussed briefly about the potential for a software company, but even though he held patents in the past, he didn't have any strong ideas or ambition about starting this kind of company now. After months of searching for employment to no avail, he was finally on board to go down a different path. He had always worked in the corporate world and had no experience running a small business. I had more confidence in him than he did in himself.

And I knew what to do. I grew up with an extended family of entrepreneurial businesses, from residential and commercial property management to van conversions, tavern operations, event planning, equipment and U-Haul rentals, and general building contracting. I could feel it in my bones. My husband, not so much – at least not at first.

I was interested in finding something that was already established. I didn't think we had the luxury of time to build a business from scratch like my family and I had done with our retail shops. We were going to need income from the get-go with a business that was time-tested.

...for the Entrepreneur

To my surprise, Michael was finally all ears. After a year, this layoff was starting to eat away at my ever-so-laid-back husband. He admitted that he was starting to feel depressed about his career. He had finally accepted that he was ready to head in another direction. Doing what we had always done in the past may have worked before, as far as job-seeking goes, but was producing no results for us this time.

After the wedding and my subsequent layoff, we still had some capital to invest in a business from our rainy-day fund. I looked on my own a bit at what businesses were for sale on some of the business-brokerage web sites. Because of our time constraint, I contacted a few business brokers and chose one. We searched throughout North Carolina, looking at businesses that appealed to us. We investigated a dry cleaner (an owner with antiquated equipment who refused to show us his books), a Dairy Queen (in a high-crime area), a Subway (in a low-traffic area), a moving company (which withdrew from the market just before we visited the facility), and a garden/patio supply store. (Their numbers were good, although a clear drop in sales was evident from the last two years.) With my previous experience in retail and a passion for this kind of home decor, I found this opportunity to be the most exciting. We visited the shop, met with the owner, and analyzed the documents, including profit-and-loss statements.

My Now...

The economy was our main concern at the time. This was a luxury-item business. I needed more time to think things over. The Iraq war was just getting started, and I did not know what kind of impact that would have on various industries and markets. We were told by our broker that another couple had also expressed interest in the business. I took that into consideration, but I didn't want that to push us into making a decision in haste.

Somewhere along the line, I had heard of SCORE (Service Corps of Retired Executives), a non-profit supported by the Small Business Administration, and wondered if they might be able to help us. I had never used their services before. I needed someone to play devil's advocate with us. I told my broker that we would speak with them. I created a presentation for SCORE and arranged a meeting. Michael and I discussed the pros and cons of this particular business with the two SCORE volunteers, and then we headed home.

We continued to discuss the business amongst ourselves, analyzing every document provided to us. However, we quickly learned that the other couple reviewing the business presented an offer that was accepted. At first, I thought I was okay with it, but then the disappointment set in. Even so, I never gave up hope. I felt that there was something else out there – but not necessarily in North Carolina. I felt that I had exhausted many of the business opportunities in the region, and approached my husband about moving out of state to

...for the Entrepreneur

an area that was not hit as hard financially as the Raleigh/Durham/RTP area. It would need to be an area that was showing continued growth. I knew that leaving our wonderful, supportive group of friends would be the hardest obstacle to overcome, but we needed to create a livelihood for ourselves.

Our North Carolina business broker was more geared toward that state, so I contacted a few different business brokers in various parts of Florida and went off in search of an opportunity. I looked at businesses in Fort Myers, Boca Raton, Hollywood, and Orlando. They were all over the map: home elderly care (a pastor-run cash business with no books to show), party rentals (they mainly dealt with a Hispanic clientele and I knew no conversational Spanish outside of "hola"), a wedding dress retail shop (this was a hot, chaotic, disorganized mess), antique shop (I got the feeling that the owner might try to compete with me from her home close by, even with a non-compete clause in place), and a property-management business (interesting concept for us, but I have to admit that I had a larger toolbox than my husband when we first met). The latter, however, did seem like a perfect match to our individual and combined set of skills. Besides, I knew that I could always buy him a larger toolbox with more tools.

To us, one of the most-promising aspects of the property-management business was the multiple revenue streams.

My Now...

There would be many ways to make money: management of the properties, rentals to tourists, tickets to Orlando theme parks, and added-on services for the investors of the properties and the clients who rented the homes and condos.

While in Orlando, I spoke with people who were running their own property-management company. Their business model was similar to the one we would follow. They explained the value of this business in more detail. Also, they explained that the average property-management business owner typically operated it for a few years and then sold it at a nice profit, considering the growth it had achieved. This appealed to both of us. Michael and I enjoy options. I also met with some of the vendors with whom we would contract. I visited the houses that we would potentially manage. Increasingly, it felt like something we could implement. I drove back to North Carolina with a plan in my hand.

We reviewed all of the documents provided to us. I contacted my parents, who were business owners themselves for years. I wanted to get their input. Was this a good idea? We also met with friends who operated their own business, picking their brains about our new plans and listening to their feedback. In addition, we visited SCORE once again with our plans and documents. They remembered us from the last presentation regarding the garden and patio business. The SCORE volunteers were intrigued by the setup of this business.

...for the *Entrepreneur*

We would be purchasing the management contracts on 20 pool homes and condos in the Kissimmee, Davenport, Clermont, Florida area, otherwise known as "Four Corners," where four counties meet. The rest of the work would be up to us to develop and market our own business. They approved what we presented to them, even more so than the garden and patio business idea. They agreed that there appeared to be more opportunity for growth.

We notified the seller of the management contracts and explained that we would be putting our house up for sale in North Carolina, with the plan to move to Florida once the house closed. We developed a business plan and starting thinking about the financing of the business. Should we try to get a bank loan? How difficult would this be? We had a good plan, projections, and skills, but we would later find out that banks simply weren't lending money that easily, even in those days before the Great Recession. Once again, that rainy-day fund would come in handy. Goodbye North Carolina, hello Sunshine State!

My husband and I reviewed our strengths and weaknesses and tailored our roles to them. We decided that Michael would up head up the accounting aspects, while I would focus on the marketing. We would both coordinate services for the homes and condos, depending on the client or vendor type.

My Now...

For the next two years, we worked non-stop. It became our lifeblood. We completely threw ourselves into our work to make it as successful as possible. We did just about anything that needed to be done for our clients and investor owners. Would you like for us to pop open that locked bedroom door? Check. Do you need for us to fix that clogged toilet after your son decided to fill it with a whole roll of toilet paper? We're on it.

Would you like for us to remove that snake that snuck under the garage door and is currently slithering through the rental home you are staying in? Gotcha. Do we need to clean a seven bedroom home in a few hours after our "new" cleaners decide that they have a family birthday party to attend instead of showing up for work? We are there (and cleaning like mad dogs before the next guests arrive). Did Michael lean too far over into the pool one day? Yep, time for a new cell phone.

Do we have to turn back from going to a play on a Saturday night in order to do some investigative work after getting a call from a customer that the furniture in their rental home was upside down and covered in sheets upon entering the home? Consider it done. They accidentally went to the house next door. It was being remodeled and the workers had left it unlocked, so they went right in without using the key. We did miss the play that night since it was too far to drive back up to Orlando again, but at least we got this crazy mystery solved.

Within two years, we doubled the number of homes managed, and had become a well-respected husband-and-wife team in the region.

But it was time for a new direction. We were ready to expand our family, and made the difficult decision to sell the business. We were meticulous, and our clients had grown accustomed to the high level of service we provided. If we added a child to the mix, we did not know if we could continue that same level of service without our family life being affected or needing to hire extra staff. We were told early on that there was a limit to the number of homes that a husband-and-wife team could handle appropriately, and we were reaching that limit. We started doing a lot of soul searching about our life goals.

I also remembered something my fellow company owners told me on my initial visit with them – that owners typically sell that kind of business after two or three years. I knew what we had created from scratch and that there was worth in the business. I developed a 25-page presentation about our company: how it had started, where it had developed, and its future potential.

Within a few months, our business sold to a lovely couple from the United Kingdom. It was one of the easiest financial

My Now...

transactions we have ever been involved in, and one of the most profitable. We followed through in our promises for training and support for them. I am pleased to report that we continue to be friends with them to this day. This is not always the case between buyers and sellers. They thanked us repeatedly for selling them a valid, reputable business that they could continue to grow themselves. Some friends of theirs had also bought into property management with another seller around the same time that they had bought our business, and their friends found themselves empty-handed. Their friends suffered great financial and emotional losses as a result.

We were thankful for the skills we learned and improved during this period of our lives and careers. Both of us had grown considerably, professionally and personally. Although none of our friends ever believe us (because of the parties we throw and our positive interactions with others), Michael and I consider ourselves to be introverts with learned social skills. (There is a difference between being a wallflower and someone who is comfortable with being by themselves.) Operating the business forced us to keep sharpening those skills, and more. We joined professional organizations and saw the value of networking for our business. Since our owner investors lived out of state or country, they were relying on us to take care of one of their major investments, if not the biggest. Trust was key. The image we presented as professionals and the timely information we relayed to them was important. We also obtained our real estate licenses to expand the business in yet one more direction.

Fast forward to several years later after our dual layoff and we have come full circle. Michael is back working with the same company that laid him off in 2001. In 2006, he started at the Atlanta site as a worker bee software engineer, and has worked his way up to his current position as a senior manager, once again.

After a few years of staying at home with our young son by choice, I am back running a small business. I located a retail shop whose owner was burned out and selling. I took over the business in early 2011, expanding and transforming it into a more upscale home decor and furniture consignment shop.

Michael and I continue to enjoy living in the sunshine of the South and raising our son here. We are both grateful for taking our individual and collective risks in life, in between the trials and tribulations that we have endured (and boy, have some of them been doozies over the years). As I am always trying to improve upon my abilities, I am intrigued to see where my future adventures will lead me next.

A few years ago, Michael attended a management-training course in Atlanta. He came home and told me a story about what they had to do that day. They each had to talk about the one life accomplishment they were most proud of. (As he spoke, I thought he was going to say something about our son, who was an infant at the time. Or maybe about a hockey badge – a bruise – he had recently earned on the ice. Or that fact that he was once a dues-paying member of Mensa.)

I was way off. Michael explained that he started his presentation sitting down. The lecturer asked him to please stand so everyone could see him. My husband quickly noted that sitting down was part of his presentation, and then he began to tell his story. (I never expected to hear what I was about to hear.) Michael spoke about his 18-year career with a company, and how he had worked his way up within the ranks of management. Next, as he remained seated, he discussed the layoff he endured, how it impacted his life and began to erode his psyche.

At this point in his story, Michael pushed his chair back abruptly and stood up. His voice became louder and firmer. He explained how he picked himself up out of the layoff ashes. He sought out a new opportunity by taking a risk that he never would have taken if he had not been laid off. Call it his silver lining, if you must. Michael had never envisioned himself as a business owner, yet he had turned out to be a successful one through hard work, patience, and determination.

...for the *Entrepreneur*

I encourage you to take that risk by "getting off the bench" (as Mr. Mark Wiggins so eloquently and consistently states), whether it is a planned and calculated course of events and actions, or as a result of life circumstances, perhaps like what happened in our story.

Upon reflection, here are some of my inspirational and business nuggets for you:

Find your passion. I cannot emphasize this enough. If you truly love what you do, you will most likely work harder at it and the very long work days will be so much easier to handle. It won't necessarily feel like work all of the time.

Start setting aside funds immediately, or develop a plan to secure funding. This is critical for capital. The old adage that it takes money to make money is never truer than when you are starting a business.

Embrace the silver linings of life, as difficult as that might be. Adversity can be an opportunity to discover new skills, meet new people, and do things you never thought you would be doing.

Opportunities to sharpen existing skills and learn new ones are everywhere. Seek them out.

A business is always for sale. A customer from my Ohio shop once told me that whenever you start a business, you

My Now...

build it from day one as if you are going to sell it someday. I thought that was brilliant. I have done this very thing with each venture that I have operated since then. It provides a different perspective for you.

Visit your local SCORE and use their resources.

Continually stoke the fires of your ambition to get off that bench. What helps you reach goals? Short-term rewards? Then set them up so you keep moving toward getting that business started. I have a lot of people who come in to my current shop with ideas they have had about creating jewelry, crafts, etc. and selling them in my store. I encourage them to bring the items in once they are completed. It is the rare person who will actually follow through on their dreams. So far I think I have had three people actually bring items in, out of many dreamers who just talk about it.

Perseverance is one of the keys to owning a business. It may not be an easy road, but you need to keep forging through the temporary barricades that may drop in front of you. When I am in the middle of problem-solving at my business, struggling with an issue that seems huge at the time, my husband will often say to me, "A year from now, this moment will be but a blip on your radar screen." He's right. It usually is. It helps me keep things in perspective – as does my sense of humor.

...for the Entrepreneur

Form a support committee made up of fellow entrepreneurs/business owners. They can be integral in providing feedback, listening to your ideas, and helping you analyze anything from the big picture to small details, depending on their own strengths.

Have you worked in the type of business that you are thinking about starting? It is best to go into a business where you have at least some minimal skills and experience within that industry, or if you have access to people who do. If you don't have any experience within your dream business, try to get a job or internship within that industry first before stepping out on your own. It may save you time to find out it was nothing like you thought it would be. My family was in residential and commercial property management for years, so I had a good level of understanding about that kind of service.

Stay focused on your business goals and be the path leader on your life journey. Isn't that why you are thinking about getting into business after all?

Outside of being married and raising a child, I think having your own business is one of the most challenging responsibilities one can take on. You will most likely work harder than you ever have before. Will you make mistakes and have failures? Yep. But operating your own business can be one of the most exhilarating achievements in your life,

My Now...

and you will grow professionally and personally like you may not in any 9-to-5 job working for someone else. Now is the time to get in the game!

"There are two mistakes one can make along the road to truth...not going all the way, and not starting." **– Buddha**

This chapter is dedicated to my friend, Kelly Clark.

...for the Entrepreneur

My Now...

Rodney Burris

Educator, National Speaker, Youth and Family Advocate, and Entrepreneur; these are some of the words used to describe Rodney Burris. In addition to a wide range of career experience, the common thread among all his ventures is a strong desire to strengthen communities.

Mr. Burris holds a BA in Psychology from the Johns Hopkins University and an MS in Management of Nonprofit Agencies from Capella University. He is deeply rooted in neighborhood empowerment and has tutored struggling students, encouraged area leaders to become more involved in the community, and reconnected fathers with their children, advising them on parenting and life skills.

Rodney is also an avid promoter of business development and entrepreneurship. His combined knowledge of non-profit experience and business-startup has been used to assist scores of interested learners. He is also one of the featured authors of the book, *My Vision, My Plan, My NOW!*

RodneyBurris@mail.com
www.RodneyBurris.com
@RodneyCBurris

...for the Entrepreneur

What's Your Burger?

Rodney Burris

There is an old saying that goes, "An entrepreneur is someone who will work 80hrs a week to keep from working 40". Have any of you found this saying true? Your heart is in being an entrepreneur. You want to start your own business, make your own hours, and be your own boss. And you are aware that it could very well mean that you are up late (and up early), burning the candle at both ends, trying to get to where you would like to be. You have a vision, and you intend to get there. Most importantly, you do not want to punch anybody's clock – at all.

Well that is good, but to keep from spinning your wheels indefinitely with minimum return on your efforts, you need to make sure you Find Your Burger.

What does that mean? Well it's just a little metaphor I like to use when talking with entrepreneurs. In short, it means, "figure out what it is you want to do, and do it." That is so simple, so logical, and yet, it is often one that we entrepreneurs struggle with. Let me go a little deeper in explaining the analogy.

My Now...

It all started with a little place that you may have heard of before – McDonald's. Well, McDs has been a well-established part of the American landscape for decades. True enough, there are certain portions of our country that has a McDs within every square mile. Any given month out of the year, McDs could be selling a rib sandwich, ice cream and cookies in a cup, a couple of rectangled-pies, chipotle wraps or salads. They serve breakfast sandwiches, pancakes, and even a combination of them both. They could sell you a chicken nugget, or a chicken tender. They might even have orange juice, apple slices and of course a few toys on hand. McDs can sell so many things to so many people, it allows them to be a jack-of-all-trades; but this isn't no ordinary jack. That's because the adage goes, "jack of all trades...master of none." And this is where McDs has set itself apart. McDs, hate it or love it, like it or leave it, is absolutely known for one thing: hamburgers and French fries.

Okay, that may be two things, but you get my point. Despite all the salads and desserts, the breakfast items and the ice cream, McDs has mastered the art of selling hamburgers and French fries. Everything else is just complimentary.

So as you venture out into the world of self-employment, you have to avoid the common traps that befall so many promising young professionals. You have to secure who you are and why you are here.

In short, you have to find your Burger.

This chapter of the My Now book for Entrepreneurs will help you do just that. First, we will explore your entrepreneurial motivation. Next, we will discover your entrepreneurial style. Lastly, we will pinpoint the five most important aspects of running any business. So let's dig in!

Before I go any further, this might be a good time to share a definition of entrepreneur. The word has three parts; entre-pre-neur. Entre means to begin, to enter, to start something new. The second portion, pre, means before; as in pre-cursor, prepay, pre-requisite, etc. Lastly, the 'neur' part is just like adding 'er' to the ending of a word: bake + 'er' = 'one who bakes'; conduct + 'or' = 'one who conducts'. Simply put, an entrepreneur is 'one who enters something before' other people. They have a certain 'risk-taker' mentality, and it allows them to apply the vision that they see into something tangible.

Step 1 - My Motivation: Money or Mankind

As entrepreneurs, we often have one of two reasons that motivate us: Social improvement or Economic improvement. Economically motivated startups exist primarily to make money. Traditional entrepreneurs fall into this category. Alternatively, most nonprofits, for example, are started to improve a social condition. However, there are some

My Now...

traditional companies that can exist for social reasons, and there are some nonprofits that pay some of their top employees a great deal of money. But before we make the waters murky, let's go ahead and further clarify each motivation type.

A Social entrepreneur is the one who likes to fix and/or address human ailments. They are also known as the bleeding heart. They're traditionally not in this to make money. Instead, they are in this to help. People have needs, and they want to meet those needs. The internet was founded upon such **dogma.** It was free. Based on the 1st amendment, everything about the internet was intended to be free - free to share, learn, grow and explore. Certain enterprising chaps saw an opportunity, and thus, birthed our second type of entrepreneur.

Traditional entrepreneur is what we commonly know of. These guys go out, and start a business to make money. There is money to be had, and they want to have it, and they generally feel like they know the best way to get there.

But what happens when the entrepreneur doesn't exactly know the best way to get to his end game? So many great ideas flounder in the wasteland, not because they don't get started, but they are unsure how to navigate the unknown in order to get there.

So, Step 1 in finding your burger: figure out, are you in this thing to make money, or are you in this thing to help people? Is your intent to be nonprofit, or for profit. Of course, the two often go in tandem. You can help people and still make money, and you can make money and still help people. Basically, anything you do in business has an effect on both people and your money. Let's look at the Redbox phenomenon for example. They guy who started the company was probably thinking, "You know, renting DVDs can be such a hassle. Wouldn't it be more convenient if..." and voilà, Redbox was born to help people with the convenience of renting. Alternatively, the same guy could've been thinking, "you know, there's no easy way really to rent DVDs on the same day, outside of Netflix. I bet I could make a lot of money if..." and voilà! Redbox was born. Of course, it's likely the same guy had both of these thoughts, and thus Redbox was born. However, one of them was the over-riding mentality. And it's important to know which of those you and your idea fall in. Neither is 'bad'. Both are equally as important, and of equal value. The problem lies in NOT knowing what motivates you.

Step 2: Conventional - Enterprising - Self-based

Once you know whether you are socially or economically motivated, you'll need to figure out your entrepreneurial expression: are you a Conventional, an Enterprising or a Self-based entrepreneur?

A conventional entrepreneur sees an opportunity in the world, and tries to address it. They are niche-fillers, and normally, if successful, go on to start their own company, bring in others, and grow it to meet demand. There is a well-known musical artist by the name of Shawn Carter (stage name: Jay Z). He is known for famously saying in a particular lyric, "I'm not a businessman, I'm a Business, man." Meaning, in him, people got to live, work, play; access careers as well as leisure. He saw an opportunity, filled the niche, and brought others in under him as the demand grew. He is an example of what we would call a 'Conventional Entrepreneur.

Another type of entrepreneur is the Enterprising entrepreneur. Whether the intent is to make money or to meet a social need, these folks revel simply in the idea of 'startups'. They love it. They always have a new idea, or see a new connection or possibility where others do not. The difference between these guys and folks who simply 'dream big' is the action. They have actually started something brand new, a time or two, from scratch. They may not stick around for the daily management of this idea, but are part of the initiation phases. Their interest can run the gamut. One day, they are talking about new eye glasses for runners. The next day they've developed talking children's books for

...for the Entrepreneur

seniors. Next week they've devised a system that makes the internet obsolete, and by next year you'll hear chatter about the new turnip seed that grows almost out of thin air. I exaggerate of course, but the main intention is to show that there does not need to be a common thread between any of their main ideas. Underneath it all, it may be a desire to help people, or to make money, but even these two ideas can switch in importance based on the new venture. The thrill is in the chase for these guys. Their greatest asset -- their constant innovation -- is also the source of their greatest liability -- inability to complete. Because their attention is so often diverted to something else that is just as valuable, just as needed, and just as financially viable, they are often drawn away in the whirlwind of their own wandering.

But don't get it confused, these are very necessary parts of our business and social fabric in that they provide a break from the old/monotonous/sanguine. They also provide opportunities for other highly skilled and qualified folks who simply have no desire to pioneer into no man's land, but are very good at structuring someone else's endeavors. Thus, enterprising entrepreneurs must be mindful that they keep complimentary folks around them at all times, not individuals who will play the 'yes-man' role, but individuals whose strengths and skills set equal to their own, in alternative aspects of the field (accounting, data-basing, researching, etc.).

The third of these (and by the way these are in no particular order) is the Self-based entrepreneur. This guy just basically wants to be in business for himself. The idea of having a big company with lots of employees is nice, but that is not really his main goal. He or she may work from home, or they may have a shop. They make work alone, or they may do it in conjunction with a few other folks. They may be open to the idea of growth and franchising, but all of their planning and actions support their close-core methodology. They love being an entrepreneur, making decent money (i.e., enough for their own needs as they consider it) and really are comfortable with keeping things consistent.

You may be any of these entrepreneur types. You may simply want to be your own boss. Or you may like the idea of continuously starting new ventures, as they give you an outlet and opportunity to be creative and innovative. Or you may simply have a good eye for market changes, know opportunity when you see one, and have the courage to strike when conditions are prime. Or, of course, you may be thinking you are some sort of combination of the three. Whichever you makeup, as an entrepreneur, you can be any or all of these things, but if you do not find out what your burger is, you are wasting your time and quite possibly wasting resources at the same time.

Step 3 - The 5 Ps (Product, Price, Place, Personnel and Population)

This exercise helps you narrow down your idea to its key structural elements.

Product

This is where you boil down to the basic of what your main offering is. Here's how you go about figuring this out. (You will actually need a sheet of paper). List all of the things you provide (no particular order, just list any and everything a customer can get from you). Keep going until you cannot think of anything else, but don't overly rack your brain about it -- if it takes that long before it comes to you, it's probably something that you really don't offer. Now, once you have your list, go through, one by one, and pretend you do not offer each item. Sometimes, this is best done with another person in the room. Often as entrepreneurs, we are as protective of our ideas as new parent, or better, as a client on the show, Hoarders. We protect every single little inch of our idea as essential. And to that point, here's what I would like for you to consider: There are parts of your own body, that if you lost them, you would not cease to exist. Likewise, there are parts of your company that is like the heartbeat, the brain. There are other parts that are preferred, and other parts that are essential. But only a few things can be viewed with life or death importance.

My Now...

Need a further example? If McDonalds stopped selling chicken selects, their quality brand of chicken tenders, would you notice? Some of you may. Some of you may not. If McDonalds stopped selling hamburgers and French fries, would you notice? Chances are, it would dominate the airwaves for at least the better part of two days (in the world of 24-hour news cycles, that's almost an eternity).

Figure out what you possibly can't live without. This is your burger. This is the thing that makes you tick. Go down the list, crossing out each item. If you can still live without, then it compliments your burger, but it isn't your burger. For example, let's look at Foot Locker. What's their burger? Tennis shoes (or sneakers, if you live in certain parts of the country). They also sell jerseys, t-shirts, ball caps, wrist bands, sweat bands, sweat socks, mouth guards and other athletic accessories. If they stopped selling sweat bands, would they cease to exist? What if they stopped selling sport shirts, or ball caps? Probably not. But if they removed all of the sneakers off of their walls and only sold those other items, Foot Locker, as we currently know it, would cease to exist. The same would happen if Taco Bell no longer sold the crunchy plain taco, but only their specialty items.

You may be inclined to think, "Well, once we have a product, I'll have my burger; what do we need the other Ps for?" Well, let's go back to our metaphor. McDs didn't just settle on a product (hamburger & French fries); instead they

...for the Entrepreneur

have an entire system designed to help properly market their product. They figured out early on that they would be a franchise. They knew from the beginning how they would price their product competitively. They embraced the drive thru model early on, because they understood their target market. They simplified their internal operations, so that they could provide jobs to low-income and or entry-level applicants. They began a special promotion to utilize toys and a name change of the kids' meal into something more 'palatable'.

Price

This is the commonplace argument of supply and demand. --The product you are offering, is it readily available? Can anyone find it anywhere? Or is your spot one of the few places a person can get it.

Place

This describes where you will actually be located. At home? In an office? What about near a college, or in a business park? Do you plan on being rural, or working downtown? Does your business take place in a van, or are you completely virtual. These are things you have to figure out

Personnel

This is who you hire. Who will work for you? What are you looking for? Who do you have already with you? Who do you need --- think in terms 'what skill sets are missing, versus trying to identify actual people. That way, if you need to replace anyone, it's possible. You look for the skill set, as opposed to being emotionally displaced by the departure.

Population

Who is your target demographic? Who will receive the messages about your grand opening? Who will be notified of any changes to your process? Basically, who is your customer?

For nonprofits, this may be a tricky question to answer. This is because the people who pay you for your services are different from the people you serve. By comparison, in a for profit company like a nail salon, the people that are serviced also fork out the money to pay for the service. They are a 'customer' in the traditional sense. In a nonprofit, however, the people an afterschool program serves (e.g., students of families in lower-income neighborhoods), cannot afford to pay for the services they receive. The payment comes from funders and grantmakers.

So let's be clear on this: nonprofits customers are your funders. They are paying you for a service, and they want to see the return on that investment. They give you money, and in return they want to see you actually deliver on the promise of your service: healthier families, better schools, smarter students, etc. If you say that you help people by doing a task, the people who pay you to do that task are your customers.

Promotion

This is about marketing. How will you get the word out?

Albert Einstein has been noted for making a very famous quote. It is, "If you can't explain something simply, you don't really understand it." This is the same for your 5 P's. The 5P's capture the essence of what you do, not the entire scope of everything you could possibly do. What is it that you do, at your core? This is the purpose of the 5P exercise. If asked, you should be able to say in one quick breath (i.e., either a single word or a short phrase) a response to each of those 5Ps. Let's look at some examples on the next page.

My Now...

	Foot Locker	McDs	Girl Scouts	iTunes
Product	Sneakers	Burgers	Character Building Service	Songs
Price*	Market Value	$1 - $4 Sandwich	$15 annually	$0.99 for most
Population	Everyday Athletes	Families on the Go	Parents of School-age Girls	Web browsers
Personnel	Young Adults into Athletics	Part-time / Transitional Employees	Volunteers	Tech Savvy Marketers and Engineers
Promotion	Very Little / Print Ads	Commercials	Cookies & Programs	"Buzz"
Place	In the Mall	Everywhere	Community Centers	Online

*Actual price points are not listed.

That's it. This simple exercise, completed as the last step of a three step process, will help you Find Your Burger and become the most effective entrepreneur you can be. I encourage you to copy this table and fill it in for your endeavor. Be sure to start with answering the Social/Economic question and then your CES style before moving into the 6P exercise. You should be well on your way in no time!

...for the Entrepreneur

Part 3: Process & Practice

My Now...

Isha Cogborn

Isha Cogborn is the founder of Epiphany Institute, a professional development company that specializes in helping people transition from employment to entrepreneurship with the talents and expertise they already possess. Her book, **5 Rules to Win in the Business of Being You**, is inspiring executives, entrepreneurs, students and people just like you to move beyond fear, uncertainty and confusion to walk confidently in their callings.

Isha beat the limited expectations for a teenage mother on welfare to chart a high-flying career in communications and brand management with a Fortune 40 global corporation. Isha excelled professionally, but suffered from severe work-related stress. When she was downsized at the height of the recession in 2009, Isha ordered new business cards **the very next day** and launched into entrepreneurship.

Isha's expertise has been featured in media outlets across the globe, including Cosmopolitan.com, Ebony Magazine and ABC TV. To find out how Epiphany Institute can help you close the gap between your career and your calling, visit **www.EpiphanyInstitute.com**.

...for the Entrepreneur

How to Defeat the Enemies of Entrepreneurship

Isha Cogborn

Are you naturally wired for entrepreneurship? Have you always challenged authority? Sought ways to create something new? Despised the thought of someone having control over how you spend your time, talent and energy? Or did you become an entrepreneur by necessity? Perhaps a lack of well-paying career opportunities or other life circumstances forced you to "get your hustle on."

However you got here, rest assured that one group doesn't have a definitive advantage over the other. The independent spirit that fuels people naturally bent to work for themselves can be as much of a curse as a blessing. I know this from personal experience.

The Quest for Independence

One of the first phrases I uttered as a child was, "I can do it myself!" When I launched Epiphany Institute – a personal development company for entrepreneurs – I taught myself

My Now...

how to build websites, basic graphic design, and even kept the books – a really bad move for someone who hates managing details. Oh yeah, and then there was actually doing the work that brought money in the door! I finally hit the ceiling and my business couldn't go any further unless I learned how to ask for help.

For many, independence equals freedom. Tim Ferriss, author of *The Four-Hour Work Week* may have mastered how to make millions with minimal effort, but that's a feat that most of us won't accomplish – at least not in the first few years of business. Getting a business off the ground is hard work. In fact, you'll probably put in more hours than you did working for someone else. But here's the great part about it – if you're doing something you're passionate about, you'll have a hard time tearing yourself away from it.

But if entrepreneurship is such a wonderful thing, why do so many people fail? There's an African proverb that says, "When there is no enemy within, the enemies outside cannot hurt you."

> "When there is no enemy within, the enemies outside cannot hurt you." African Proverb

Although a lack of finances, a bad business plan or competition can certainly tank a business, it is often the enemies within that lead to failure. I call them your internal opponents.

...for the Entrepreneur

There are five internal opponents to be very mindful of when it comes to your business:

1. Lack of Knowledge
2. Lack of Focus
3. Lack of Passion
4. Fear
5. Laziness and Procrastination

Lack of Knowledge

One of the greatest internal opponents for entrepreneurs is a lack of knowledge. It's even more of a challenge when you don't know what you don't know.

According to Google, information searches on its site surpassed an average of 4.7 billion each month in 2011. WorldWideWebSize.com estimates that there are at least 9.42 billion pages of information indexed online. With the push of a button on your smart phone, you can locate a source for almost anything that you want to know within minutes. Yet, many people never even take the first step toward their professional dreams, because they say they don't know where to start. How about starting with a Google search?

Every week, I discover new tools or processes to function more effectively in my business. I have also made my share of mistakes because of things that I just didn't know. It's one thing when you don't know what you don't know, but it's unacceptable when we know exactly what information we need to move forward, yet fail to seek it out.

> "My people are destroyed for lack of knowledge." – Hosea 4:6

In addition to online searches, here are five tips to help you gather the intelligence you need to succeed:

1. Talk to others who have already done what you want to do. Prepare a list of questions in advance and be respectful of their time. If the person you're approaching shares the knowledge you're asking for *as part of their business*, offer to pay them. Asking a consultant if you can pick their brain over lunch is like buying a surgeon a cup of coffee to remove your gallstones. Make an effort to connect with at least one new person each month.
2. Find out what publications and websites successful people in your industry read, what groups they belong to, and who they look to as role models and mentors. If you don't know them personally, look at who they follow on Twitter or what Facebook pages they like.
3. When you join professional organizations or networking groups, don't just hide out. Build relationships or consider volunteering in a formal capacity if your schedule allows.

4. Find online groups where information related to your efforts is routinely shared. In 2011, I started a Facebook group called ... **But I Don't Want a REAL Job!** for folks who currently have or want to start their own businesses. People from around the world convene in the group to share tips, ask questions and connect with like-minded individuals. Do searches on LinkedIn, Facebook, Google Plus or other social networking sites for groups that will meet your needs.
5. Set aside a specific time each week for professional development. Trying to take in too much at a time can lead to analysis paralysis. Be careful not to question whether or not what you're doing is right to the point that you don't do anything at all.

Lack of Focus

Another reason many businesses flounder is a lack of focus. Most entrepreneurs I know – including myself – are at least a little bit ADD. If not properly managed, you can develop what I call "squirrel syndrome" – running your business like a dog that chases every random squirrel that comes along. Take a look at your computer. If you have multiple files or applications open at one time, you just might have squirrel syndrome! Even if you're only focusing on one project, most entrepreneurs tend to devote most of their energy to the tasks they enjoy most. But what we like or even

My Now...

what we're most skilled at doing may not always be the most profitable activities to be working on at the time. And that's another reason why it's important to know when to ask for help.

Focusing on the right things for a successful business begins with your vision. Where do you want to go? Once you're clear on that, create goals that will get you there. Be sure your goals are SMART – specific, measurable, attainable, relevant and time-bound. At the specified deadline you ought to be able to clearly answer yes or no about whether or not you met the goal. If you can't, it's not specific enough.

> Focusing on the right things for a successful business begins with your vision.

In order to have time and energy to carry out the activities necessary to reach your goals, you may need to let go of some things.

Take Action:

Make a list of everything you're involved in, including your job, parenting, church committees, volunteer activities, and even social commitments.

Next, circle every activity that is a requirement. Now write your circled items on a separate piece of paper.

For every uncircled item on the first piece of paper, honestly assess if continuing those activities helps or hinders reaching your business goals. If it's a hindrance, plan your exit strategy from these activities. Don't just drop the ball if you've made commitments – keeping your reputation in tact is critical.

When a fighter is training for a title bout, they must go to great lengths to protect themselves from distractions that could undermine their progress. The medical definition for distraction is "diversion of the attention" – not "time wasters" or "futile activities. A distraction could be anything that diverts your attention away from achieving your business goals – no matter how worthy of an activity it may be.

Because you're good at what you do, people will always ask for your help. That could be at work, at church, in the community, and especially among your family and friends. Don't get me wrong, I'm not telling you to become completely selfish and refuse to do anything that doesn't benefit you and the advancement of your business. But what I am saying is that if all the extra activities are keeping you from completing your primary assignment, something has to change.

Lack of Passion

The third reason many businesses fail is a lack of passion. Are you involved in your business just because someone told you it would be lucrative, or do you really have a heart for what you're doing?

I see this a lot in the direct sales and network marketing industry. According to the Direct Selling Association, there were 15.6 million people involved in multi-level and direct marketing companies in the United States alone in 2011. For many, these business opportunities present a chance to bring in a few hundred extra dollars a month to upgrade their lifestyle, save for a major expense or to close the gap between shrinking earnings and rising expenses. But there are others who sign up looking for their golden ticket out of an unfulfilling career.

Here's a recipe for disaster...

You sign up for a business selling products or services that you're really not excited about, but because you're convinced it's something that "everyone needs" you believe it will sell itself. But the products don't sell themselves. In fact, you're spending countless hours following up with prospective customers and business partners. When you discover you're not making money as quickly as you thought you would, the excitement wears off and it begins to feel like just another job. Before long, you've given up on the business and you're not any closer to the financial freedom you were seeking. In fact, you may have even lost money.

...for the Entrepreneur

Please don't misunderstand me – I'm not against direct marketing companies in general. However, I find it disappointing that many people don't do a better job of finding business opportunities that are more closely aligned with their passions or ultimate goals. If you're considering an entrepreneurial venture – especially if it's on top of a "real job," make sure you enjoy it. If you don't, the chances that you'll put in the effort and long-term commitment necessary to be financially successful are nearly non-existent.

Passion is a powerful commodity. Passion is the stuff that sustains you when you're exhausted and broke. And if you're not passionate about your business, it can be very difficult to move forward.

When you're focused and passionate about your business, you won't give up until you find success.

Fear

> When you're focused and passionate about your business, you won't give up until you find success.

Fear is the ultimate "F" word. It's nasty enough to keep many from ever even taking a step towards making their dreams come true. Overcoming fear requires a process of unraveling toxic thoughts. And it begins with finding out just what you're afraid of. For most, it's the fear of failure. But for me and plenty of other entrepreneurs, it's actually the fear of success that can keep us paralyzed. Will people expect more

My Now...

of me than I'm able to deliver? Will the people around me change?

Whether it's a fear of failure or a fear of success you're experiencing, it all really comes back to a fear of the unknown: You don't know what's going to happen and it scares you. The secret to getting around that hurdle is to deconstruct your fear. What exactly are you afraid of and what will happen if those fears are realized?

Take Action:

1. Make a list of everything you're afraid of that's hindering you from moving forward in your business.
2. For each item you've written, ask yourself what might happen if that fear is realized? If that happens, then what? Then what? Continue down this path until you can't go any further.
3. Next, make a list of all of the good things that are possible as a result of you moving forward. Keep writing until you can't think of anything else.
4. Take a look at both lists and ask yourself, "Does pursuing the possible successes warrant what I may stand to lose?" If the answer is yes, keep going. If the answer is no, look for ways to minimize your risks.

Remember, the greater the risk, the greater the reward. Playing it safe isn't the road that leads to greatness. Be smart, not safe.

...for the *Entrepreneur*

Laziness and Procrastination

The freedom of being your own boss is a beautiful thing. You're not punching anybody's clock. No one is setting arbitrary goals that you're forced to meet to get a raise or promotion. And in many cases, you have the ability to tailor your schedule to accommodate your personal responsibilities and interests. But freedom without accountability can lead to laziness and procrastination.

> Freedom without accountability can lead to laziness and procrastination.

Here are a few tips to keep you productive:

1. Create a Timeline with Key Milestones

Yes, there are lots of unknowns when launching a startup, but you'll get a lot more done even with a timeline that changes than if you don't have one at all.

My freshman year of college, I experienced a major unplanned event – I had a baby. But before I would even take a pregnancy test, I had to have a plan. If I was pregnant, I'd take the second semester off, have the baby in May, go to summer school at the community college in June, and pack up the baby and head back to campus in August, only a half semester behind. Great plan, right? But it didn't quite happen that way. I had my son in May, registered for classes at the community college, but then had

My Now...

to drop them because I didn't have transportation. And instead of sitting out for a semester, it took a year and a half to get back in school. I graduated two years later than planned, but I still finished. If I didn't have a timeline in front of me – even though it changed – I would have had nothing to work towards and probably wouldn't have finished college. Force yourself to create a plan.

2. **Give Yourself Weekly Performance Reviews**

When you worked for someone else, there were consequences for not getting your work done on time. But now that you're your own boss, you have to create that same accountability for yourself.

Try to have set working hours and use your timeline to help you set your priorities for each year, each quarter, each month, each week, and each day. I have a tool I created for my clients that I also use to be realistic about how much I can really accomplish in a given day and it makes me ask myself at the end of each day what I did well and what I could have done better. If you'd like a copy, email me at info@CoachIsha.com.

3. **Make it Bigger than You**

It's easy to get complacent about your business when all you're thinking about is how it impacts you. Ask yourself, "Who wins when I win?" When you're successful, who will

...for the *Entrepreneur*

benefit? How will they benefit? How can you use that to motivate you when you're ready to give up or waste time working on something that's not really important?

When Twitter was founded, did they know it would be an outlet to spark political revolutions like the Arab Spring? Probably not. How can your business change the world? Or change an individual who then can go out and change the world? When you focus on how the work you're doing (or procrastinating about doing) will make a positive impact on others, it ought to compel you to spring into action.

Running a successful business begins and ends with you. No matter how great your idea is or how many investors you have, if you allow internal opponents like a lack of knowledge, lack of focus or passion, fear or laziness and procrastination to keep you on the ropes, winning is a long shot.

> Running a successful business begins and ends with you.

Entrepreneurship is not an excuse for operating without a plan or giving less than everything you have within you. And never forget that people are counting on you to win, so stay in the fight!

My Now...

Lisa Harrington

Lisa Harrington is the co-owner and president of Bonitas International, a specialty fashion accessory company. She began her business in 2003 and quickly grew it to a multi-million dollar enterprise in the first 3 years. Lisa has a passion for creating functional products that are also fabulous. She resides in Cincinnati, Ohio and can be reached at **LHarrington@bonitasinternational.com**.

...for the Entrepreneur

From Bedsides to Beads

Lisa Harrington

Ten years ago, when I first started my business, I did not think I had the skills or characteristics of a successful entrepreneur.

Happily, I found that I was wrong!

Although I did not have a business background or much experience outside of my nursing career, I found that I did have the attributes that lead to great success with starting and growing a business.

It started off quite simply.

Ten years ago, I was working as a highly specialized Pediatric Nurse in a major children's hospital. I was making a very good salary with great benefits. I was really good at my job and I enjoyed it. One day, my daughter made me a beaded necklace to wear to work, which I used to display my work ID.

My co-workers loved the idea of a colorful, happy necklace to use instead of the work-issued, boring lanyard.

My Now...

Many of my colleagues offered to buy the necklaces and even suggested I make more and sell them to others.

I didn't know it at the time, but this would be the beginning of a whole new career and life direction for me. My sister-in-law convinced me that, together, we could turn this into a successful business.

A nurse turned entrepreneur? I was a bit overwhelmed at the thought. Consequently, I began my journey with much fear and apprehension. The thought of risking the life-savings of my family, my business partner's family and a loan from my in-laws was daunting. But, with much support and encouragement, I was able to push past my fears and jump right in to entrepreneurism.

Pushing past your fears is not an easy undertaking. One thing that has helped me is the knowledge that often times, when people do not understand something or are faced with an unknown; we tend to fill that void of information with fear. In that place of fear, we may imagine an outcome or answer much worse than the truth or reality. Just the awareness of this phenomenon itself is tremendously helpful in managing my fears and overcoming many hurdles along the way. It drives me to replace the unknown with as much information as possible so the void doesn't stay open long enough for fear to become all-consuming and immobilizing.

...for the *Entrepreneur*

How do you get the information you need to overcome fear?

We can't possibly be experts at everything. We excel in certain areas and for the rest...we may need some help.

The challenge for some, however, can be asking for it.

That is a skill I have had to work very hard to develop as an entrepreneur. Luckily, I am a person who always likes "to know" and that has been important in getting over my discomfort in asking for help. For me learning is something I have always found essential and exciting. Even as a nurse, I was always asking questions. I found the more I understood about the body; how it works, how disease processes developed and were treated, etc., the better nurse and advocate I became for my patients and families. It may seem like a stretch at first, but that basic "need to know" has helped me tremendously as an entrepreneur. I found that I must always ask questions, ask again for clarity and if I think I need additional information...I'll ask some more!

Through this tireless questioning, researching and much trial and error, I essentially taught myself much of what I needed to know about basic product development and the oversight of overseas manufacturing for my fashion accessories. It seems like a far cry from nursing, doesn't it? However, the constant need for information I gained as a nurse is exactly what prepared me for the challenges of

My Now...

running a jewelry business. I am not an expert at every single aspect of the manufacturing process, such as import laws, logistics, etc., but, I quickly gained enough of an understanding to make important decisions and to find the people that *are* experts in those areas.

For an entrepreneur, or any businessperson, the ability to seek help and take it when necessary is essential to success. Perhaps just as important, is the willingness to be open-minded to creative strategies and input.

Again, this is not a skill one necessarily learns in a business school.

In my first career, I used creative strategies to help children and families comply with treatment plans. As an entrepreneur, I encourage idea sharing and brain-storming. Along with my partner, we promote an environment of transparency so our team can feel empowered with a full understanding of our company's position and direction. We've found that truly engaging our employees leads to an amazing amount of input, feedback and commitment from our team. Our business is thriving today because of our eagerness to entertain the many different ideas and approaches to problem-solving we've received. These strategies have applied to everything from small product solutions to financing million dollar buys.

...for the *Entrepreneur*

Have we made mistakes along the way? Absolutely. Very early in our business we decided to call mistakes "opportunities" or "learnings" because that is what they truly are. When outcomes are not what we expected, we look at that as the perfect opportunity to learn something new and to change what we do as a company. The road has not been easy...at one point in our first 5 years of business, after a particularly rough stretch, my partner and I jokingly said, "Ok, we are tired of learning now!"

I would not be honest if I said it doesn't get frustrating overcoming these "learning opportunities". However, we have found that we can find something of value to use as a tool to move forward from every single circumstance, no matter how seemingly useless a mistake or turn of events can be. The saying, "If you keep doing the same things, you will get the same results," is very true indeed. When I consider how far we have come and how much we have grown as individuals and as a company in the past ten years, I often reminisce on how we used to do things. We sometimes say things like, "Can you believe we ever survived doing it that way?" or "We do it so much better now, what were we thinking back then?" That, as I often say, is the whole point. We don't do things that way any longer and we survive because we **change, grow** and **learn** from things that have not gone exactly as planned. What we did early in our business worked at the time and when it didn't, we took the

My Now...

opportunity to change and improve what wasn't working well.

During these ten years of owning my business, I have had the great pleasure of meeting many successful entrepreneurs. Although I have yet to meet a nurse turned entrepreneur, I have met several with varied backgrounds, careers and experiences. Many of the people I've met had strong business backgrounds with (and without) business degrees. I've met just as many entrepreneurs who began like me...with a passion for a product or service, the courage to push past fears, the willingness to accept guidance, the drive to seek creative solutions and the initiative to take advantage of opportunities to grow through change.

...for the *Entrepreneur*

My Now...

Sharon A. Myers

Sharon A. Myers is the Chief Marketing Officer at Visionary Engineering & Services LLP. She has more than 10 years of experience in providing marketing and business development support and services to entrepreneurs, small- and mid-sized business owners.

She is also the Executive Director of Moovin4ward Presentations, a youth empowerment company that facilitates leadership and success workshops for high school and college students around the country. She is the co-author of *Mapping Your Journey to Success: Six Steps for Personal Planning* and co-developer of the student program, **Journey to Success: Personal Success Strategic Plan (PSSP) Program**. Sharon is also the author of *My Vision, My Plan, My NOW; Slumber Party, Critical Competence,* and *90 Tips for the First 90 Days*.

sharon@moovin4ward.com

www.Moovin4ward.com

www.Journey2Success.com

@sharonamyers

...for the *Entrepreneur*

The Right Stuff

Sharon A. Myers

You've done it! You developed the greatest product ever! Let's say you've developed a revolutionary spray-on hair growth product, which we'll call Mo-Grow. All the consumer has to do is to spray it on a bald area, and hair will begin to grow within minutes. Your target market for the new product will be EVERYONE!

Who wouldn't want to grow hair on their balding areas? I'm guessing the countless number of people who do NOT have balding areas.

As a matter of fact, these people, those already with an abundance of hair, could probably care less about your product. Then there are those who do have balding spots, but aren't willing to spend money to do anything about it. Clearly, EVERYONE is not your target market.

I have spent a great many of years counseling the would-be entrepreneur. Many times I have to play devil's advocate and ask the hard questions, as this is the best way to ensure that the entrepreneur is ready to move forward. I'll start by asking, "What will you sell?" That is the easiest question. Most all of my clients would answer this one with ease, detail, and passion.

My next question is, "Who cares?"

"Huh?" is generally the response.

Who cares what services or products you have to offer? Or better put, what person, or preferably, group of people will most likely PURCHASE the services or products you have to offer? To be even more specific, who is the right customer?

If you're targeting everyone, you are not really targeting anyone. A successful business is capable of providing the right product, at the right price, sold at the right place, to the right customer. When you figure out who actually cares about what you offer, you've identified your right customer.

The Right Customer

Most people believe that marketing is only about networking, advertising or promotions. But it's actually much, much broader than that. It's about knowing exactly what a *particular* customer, the right customer, cares about, needs, or wants.

Let's dig deeper. Who cares about a dishwashing liquid that literally erases grease off pans without scrubbing?

...for the *Entrepreneur*

Apparently, not people who are watching sport channels; because I've yet to see a commercial for dishwashing liquid on any of them. That's not to say that people who watch Sports Center don't wash dishes. But chances are low that anyone, while watching their favorite game, race or sport news, is thinking about or concerned with greasy dishes. I'm also guessing that they don't care about absorbent diapers, because I don't recall seeing those commercials either.

Why? Aren't there Dads watching Sports Center? Aren't there Moms watching ESPN? Let's be honest with this... there are probably way more men watching the sport channels; and washing dishes or purchasing diapers is probably not high on the "to do" list for most of them. So spending money to advertise these items on sport channels might be a waste, because you aren't targeting the right customer.

However, as sexist as this might sound, it would probably be better to advertise on channels or during shows that a vast majority of women or mothers are watching, such as OWN or Lifetime. And you'd really hit gold if your commercial were played during the day when the "at-home" mothers or fathers are washing dishes and/or changing diapers.

Here's another example. Let's say I have a pizza business that delivers on weekends. I'm certain that one of my targeted customers would be the sport buff who wants to

My Now...

spend their weekends watching the games, not cooking and/or moving from their Lazy Boy in front of the television.

If I wanted this group of sport buffs to come into my pizza restaurant I might promote that I have multiple 50" flat screen televisions with all of the games playing all the time. I'd also promote that my place is a "kid free zone" where my customers could hang out with their buddies to relax to enjoy the game with no thought of dishes or diapers. I know this because I've done some research on what this group cares about.

Don't get me wrong, surely everyone loves pizza! Kids love pizza! But it would be very expensive to try to satisfy both kids and sport buffs; because they don't care about the same things. If I determined that kids or families with kids were my targeted customers, I would get rid of the large screens televisions and would fill the place with games, activities and FUN! Why? Because fun is what kids care about.

Do you see where I'm going with this?

Marketing your business is about how you position it to satisfy your market's need—NOT EVERYONE'S NEEDS, but your targeted customer—the right customer.

...for the Entrepreneur

The Right Stuff

I pride myself on making spectacular omelets. With a family of five, however, it would be difficult to satisfy them all with just one recipe. They all want the "right stuff" according to them. The right stuff for my husband would be lots of green peppers, onions and mushrooms, very light on the seasonings, with a touch of shredded cheese. The right stuff for my youngest daughter is light cheese, turkey sausage, and my special seasoning blend. The right stuff for my son is turkey sausage, turkey bacon and red chili peppers. And the right stuff for my oldest daughter is cheese, cheese and more cheese. Since I know exactly what they want or care about, I can be sure to put the right combination together to ensure they eat every bite and always come back for more.

After you have identified the right customer and learned all that you can about their needs or wants, you can then create a marketing mix—the right stuff—of all the goodies they want.

There are four critical elements that make up the marketing mix, also known as the Four Ps of Marketing:

1) _Product_. The right product to satisfy the needs of your targeted customer.
2) _Price_. The right product offered at the right price.
3) _Place_. The right product at the right price available in the right place to be bought by customers.

4) <u>Promotion</u>. The right method of informing potential customers of the product, its price and its place.

Each of the four Ps is a variable you control in creating the marketing mix that will attract customers from your targeted market to your business. Your marketing mix should be something you pay careful attention to because the success of your business depends on it. As an entrepreneur, you must determine how to use these variables just right to achieve your profit potential.

Customer research is a key element in building an effective marketing mix. Your knowledge of your target market and your competitors will allow you to offer a product or service that will appeal to customers and avoid costly mistakes.

Product

"Product" refers to the goods and services you offer to your customers. Apart from the physical product itself, there are elements associated with your product that customers may be attracted to, such as the way it is packaged. If it's a product, the packaging must catch the eye of the right customer and be branded to fit the solution of the product. If it's a service or place, the branding should match the customer's expectations.

...for the Entrepreneur

Consider our pizza place that's filled with sport paraphernalia, hot wings, and multiple televisions playing sports versus a pizza place with loud games, toy prizes and teenage employees dressed in animal costumes.

Your product's appearance, function, and service make up what the customer is actually buying. Other product attributes include quality, features, options, support, warranties, and brand name.

Price

"Price" refers to how much you charge for your product or service. Determining your product's price can be tricky and even frightening. Many entrepreneurs feel they must absolutely have the lowest price around. So they begin their business by creating an impression of bargain pricing.

However, this may be a signal of low quality and not part of the image you want to portray. Consider the difference between the Honda commercial that boast an economy car versus the Cadillac that boasts class and prestige. Consider Wal-Mart versus Target... I want low prices everyday while my girlfriend will pay more at Target to avoid the rustle and bustle.

Your pricing approach should reflect the appropriate positioning of your product or service in the market and result in a price that covers your cost per item and includes a profit margin. If you are too greedy with a high price, you may price yourself out of the market. If you are too timid with a low price, you might make it too impossible to grow.

You can follow a number of alternative pricing strategies. Some price decisions may involve complex calculation methods, while others are intuitive judgments.

Here are four common pricing strategies.

1) *Cost-plus:* Adds a standard percentage of profit above the cost of producing a product.
2) *Value-based:* Based on the buyer's perception of value (rather than on your costs).
3) *Competitive*: Based on prices charged by competing firms for competing products.
4) *Going-rate:* A price charged that is the common or going-rate in the marketplace.

Whatever your price may be, ultimately it must cover your costs, contribute to your image by communicating the perceived value of your product, counter the competition's offer, and avoid deadly price wars. Remember, price is the one "P" that generates revenue, while the other three "P's" incur costs. Effective pricing is important to the success of your business.

Place

"Place" refers to the distribution channels used to get your product to your customers. What your product is will greatly influence how you distribute it. Businesses that create or assemble a product will have two options: selling directly to consumers or selling to a vendor.

Direct Sales

Let's go back to our Mo-Grow spray. How would we distribute it? We might consider direct sales through retail, door-to-door, mail order, online, on-site, or some other method. An advantage of direct sales would be the contact we gain by meeting customers face to face. With this contact we can easily detect market changes that occur and adapt to them. We will also have complete control over our product range, how it is sold, and at what price.

Direct sales may be a good place to start when the supply of your product is limited or seasonal. For example, direct sales for many home-produced products can occur through home-based sales, markets, and stands.

Reseller Sales

We may decide to sell through an intermediary such as a wholesaler or retailer who will resell our product. Doing this may provide us with a wider distribution than selling direct while decreasing the pressure of managing our own distribution system. Additionally, we may also reduce the storage space necessary for inventory.

One of the most important reasons for selling through an intermediary is access to customers. In many situations, wholesalers and retailers have customer connections that would not be possible to obtain our own.

You may decide to have a combination of all the distribution methods. Whatever you decide, choose the method which you believe will work best for you and the right customer.

Promotion

"Promotion" refers to the advertising and selling part of marketing. This is the part that most people associate with marketing. It is how you let people know what you've got for sale. The purpose of promotion is to get people to understand what your product or service is, how they can benefit from it, and why they should want it.

Knowing what your customer cares about helps you to craft the perfect message to get their attention via an appropriate channel. When you have more than one type of customer, which is also possible, then you'll need more than one message using more than one channel.

Your message must be consistent with your overall marketing image, get your target audience's attention, and elicit the response you desire.

Here are a few of the key promotional channels:

- *Advertising* channels include promoting your product or service via radio, television, print materials, websites, or word of mouth.
- *Public Relations* channels usually focuses on the role of a salesperson in your communication plan, where the salespersons can tailor the message to customers and are very important in building relationships.
- *Discount* channels are special offerings designed to encourage purchases. These promotions might include free samples, coupons, contests, incentives, loyalty programs, prizes, and rebates.
- *Personal Sales* channels may include attending or participating in trade shows, educating customers through seminars, setting up displays at public events, and networking socially in online groups.

Your target audience may be more receptive to one method than another, so include a variety in your marketing mix to ensure that you attract the right customer.

My Now...

Final Thought

With more than 312 million people in the United States, you really don't need all of them to be your customers. Having a well-defined target market is critical to establishing your marketing strategy and growing your business. The four P's—product, price, place and promotion—work together to ensure that you attract the "right customer" with the "right stuff." Although selecting an effective mix for the market will take time and effort, it will pay off as you satisfy what your customers care about.

...for the Entrepreneur

My Now...

Michael Tucker

Michael Tucker is an international speaker, author, trainer and consultant as well as the founder and CEO of Social Mobile Buzz, a marketing and communications company specializing in turning inspiring professionals and companies into champion brands through the use of integrated traditional and digital marketing solutions. Social Mobile Buzz represents small, mid-sized and large clients in the corporate, non-profit, and government sectors. Michael earned his bachelor's degree in Retail Management from the University of South Carolina and a master's in Human Relations from the University of Oklahoma. He is also one of the featured authors of the book, *My Vision, My Plan, My NOW!*

Michael currently lives in Tucson, Arizona with his wife Ellen.

MrMichaelTucker.com

Twitter @mrmichaeltucker

michael@socialmobilebuzz.com

...for the Entrepreneur

Let's Make A Deal to Not Chase the Deal

Michael Tucker

Early last year I had one of the highest grossing months of my marketing career. I was very excited. Throughout that month my smile was bigger and brighter than ever. I walked taller, I felt "secure," I was confident and I was generous to friends and strangers alike. I was experiencing success and I felt the overflow of abundance that I had often heard others speak of. All that month I lived as a wealthy man because I felt wealthy.

Then, I had a thought...

Doubt enters as my mind reels, "Landing this deal was great...**but**...how will I do it again? Where will my next 'big deal' come from? How should I go about chasing it down?"

The more I repeated these questions in my mind, the less I was able to experience the amazing feelings I mentioned above; the less grateful I became; and the more fearful and worried I was. The wind had left my sail and I went from feeling like a million bucks to feeling like I had to survive or

My Now...

"just hold on a little while longer." In a matter of days I had gone from experiencing the bliss of my greatest success to coddling my fears. I even got the great idea to hold an image in my mind of a man doing everything he could to keep from slipping off a life raft in the middle of the ocean. How inventive and how counter-productive!

After slowly watching my feelings of abundance erode over a relatively short amount of time, I came to the conclusion that I did not like returning to the "familiar" feelings of fear from the past. I wanted to experience abundance again. It was as if somehow my success was forcing deeply rooted fears of lack and uncertainty to the surface of my mind.

Has this ever happened to you? I would suggest that this experience is not uncommon in our society. Have you ever wondered why famous athletes, actors, or musicians fall into self-destructive behavior after their big payday? Have you ever wondered what would inspire a rapper like Notorious B.I.G. to write a song entitled "More Money More problems?" Some say that large amounts of money or fame change people. I would suggest just the opposite. These things don't change us. Instead, they more aggressively point out what's already going on inside of us.

If you are angry and emotionally unsettled as a poor person you will be even angrier and more unsettled with money. Conversely, if you are generous when you have little money you will be even more generous when you have large amounts of it. The latter explains why people who come into large sums of money often give it all away. Note: Balance can be a good thing.

Until coming in contact with such a large amount of money that I had earned on my own merits, I did not realize just how much fear and uncertainty I was holding in my subconscious mind. I also did not realize how this fear sometimes managed to seep into my everyday decision making process without me even knowing.

Have you ever gone shopping with plenty of money in your pocket or bank account and chosen to purchase a brand of product that was less prestigious than the one you actually wanted just to save a few dollars? Some call this being thrifty. I disagree. Being thrifty is getting what you want at the price you want. Being controlled by fear is choosing the lesser brand you *don't want* because somewhere deep in your subconscious mind, you believe that by paying an extra dollar for the Crest toothpaste you actually want will land you in the poor house.

Fortunately, over the years, I have attended a number of personal development programs and read several books about spirituality and being self-aware, so when my mind started challenging my success, I was able to take a stand.

These teachings helped me realize that my thoughts were leading me in a direction I did not want to go. Then in that instance a flash of truth hit me.

I was reminded that wholeness and abundance had always been my natural state. If this were not true how could I know the difference between abundance and poverty? If I had never experienced an abundance of health how could my body know to heal itself when it gets a cut or catches a cold? To my knowledge, I've never had to remind myself to breath of keep my heart beating? Have you?

We live in a world of abundance just as fish live a world of water. Acquiring this new money was amplifying my emotions associated with the truth of abundance. It also happened to trigger some limiting beliefs I was holding on to as well. The great thing about realizing this was concluding that if an external event could trigger such an internal mental experience and that's what caused me to feel abundant, I could choose to recreate the experience of abundance anytime by simply shifting my behavior, thoughts, and emotions. I could experience abundance regardless of whether I had landed a new deal or not. Feeling good is critical to entrepreneurial growth. Feeling success always breeds actualized success.

So here's what I did.

I began to recall all of the experiences that bought me to my current place. In that moment I choose to feel a deep appreciation and gratitude for these experiences. I choose to love and honor being exactly where I was. I stopped my conscious mind from asking about where my "next deal" would come from and decided to ask "Why was my next deal a success?"

My response?

"My next deal was a success because gratitude allowed me to feel at peace. My focus was clear and I took immediate action when I received inspiration."

Did you notice how I addressed my future success as if it had already taken place? Doing this helped create a new context for my thoughts. Instead of wondering if I would be successful in the future, I instead began to place my thoughts on positive actions that had created the success I was currently experiencing in my mind. By simply asking a better question, I changed my entire perspective. What questions could your rephrase in order to see the world newly?

After my thought process had been adjusted and I was once again feeling at peace with myself and the world, I went to work "creating space for new opportunities." I'd like to take a moment to draw attention to the fact that I did not move forward with a new endeavor or strategy session or action until my mind was clear. This only took a matter of seconds and is important to note. When our mind is in a state of lack or fear and our emotions are low, it is next to impossible to identify with the opportunities waiting for us, even though they are literally everywhere. We are simply blind to them.

I'd also like to point out the fact that I consciously chose to "create space for new opportunities" as opposed to simply throwing money at new marketing initiatives. Anyone can run an ad campaign or hire a marketing professional (people hire me all the time). However, if your mindset is weak or steeped in fear and lack the results of your efforts will follow suit. "Get your mind right" first, as my dad used to say, by adopting an attitude of gratitude then you can take an empowered action step (like hiring me). Calming the mind clears the pathway for *the right* type of new business to present itself.

Have you ever had a friend with a negative attitude and nothing ever seemed to go right for her? Regardless of the externalities she claims to be her problem (the spouse, clients, IRS, weather etc.) you and I both know that her acceptance of doubts and disempowering beliefs is what keeps her success at bay. This truth is no different when it comes to entrepreneurship. Attitude truly is everything. It determines your state of being and assigns a measure of quality to the actions you carry out. The more positive, proactive and generous your attitude, the greater the perceived and/or experienced quality of your actions.

As a part of my conscious effort to "Create space for new opportunities" I choose to genuinely consider how my marketing company could make a greater, more meaningful contribution in the lives of stakeholders touched by my firm (clients, partners, venders, community, etc.) beyond simply providing a good service.

I decided to take the following actions; develop new systems to enhance the effectiveness of my current efforts, increase my level of focus and engagement within key niches, add staff, and take steps to become more customer centered by gaining deeper customer insight.

Systems Development

In order for businesses to run successfully and achieve scalability or growth, systems and business processes must be created and implemented throughout the organization. Creating systems allows the business owner to accomplish more and provide better customer care because work efforts don't fall completely on his/her shoulders. They can now be delegated. When documented systems allow tasks to be delegated, the business owner, is free to focus on the direction and growth of the business as opposed to only doing the work of the business.

My Now...

In other words, systems keep business owners from simply trading time for dollars and having a nervous breakdown. Systems also build the foundational infrastructure needed to create jobs and hire others. Michael Gerber, one of the world's leading authorities on business development, discusses the importance of organizational processes and systems in great detail in his book "The E Myth Revisited." According to Michael, in addition to a primary aim, companies need organizational, people management, and marketing systems.

Some of the internal systems and process we perfected within our company included; streamlining our customer onboarding process, billing practices and hiring strategy. Structuring our systems and process to be more efficient in these areas has allowed us to increase productivity and hire additional workers.

Focused Engagement on Key Niches

After refining a few basic systems to support business development, I revisited my business plan and made a strategic effort to hone in on the types of organizations I enjoyed working with and/or seemed to be a good fit for my firm. In the past I would take almost any job that came my way. Focusing our efforts and choosing a niche meant being willing to pass some opportunities to other firms or consultants.

...for the *Entrepreneur*

For example, I used to host social media marketing classes that trained small business owners how to use Facebook and other social media sites. I concluded these classes a year after starting them because I was beginning to work one-on-one with clients as a consultant. Before I choose to deepen my focus I would often end up working with new start-ups whom at the time did not have the need or means to investment in private consulting. After I focused on new key niches (nationally certified women/minority-owned mid-sized businesses, social enterprises, government and corporate firms) I passed these clients on to social media classes and groups held by others in my city. Thereby, ensuring they maintained a steady stream of customers and managing my time more effectively.

Create Jobs

Adding new teammates to my organization was a big deal for me. It meant that my business was evolving and I would be required to think beyond myself and my needs alone. As an Air Force officer in my former life, I was accustomed to leading hundreds of people, both military and civilian. Leadership skills weren't my concern. However, I was concerned about how I would afford to pay new team members.

My approach to hiring was very methodical. My very first "employees" were actually two interns from the University of

My Now...

Arizona. They worked for free in exchange for college credit and letters of recommendations. Interestingly enough, I am now helping one of my former interns find funding and support for a start-up company he and some roommates launched. Their company, Patheer.com, helps people methodically plan their career paths by giving them access to closely-held insight from professionals that have already succeeded.

Next, I hired a virtual assistant, and a number of virtual team members abroad to help work on projects. This was not without a few challenges but I made it work. If you're an "American jobs" only person, I would challenge you to expand your perspective. Without these workers I could have never afforded to take my businesses to a level which allowed me to actually hire Americans. More importantly, I was able to provide meaningful well-paying work for a number of incredible people with limited job opportunities.

After working with a virtual work force for nearly a year I hired an amazing assistant in my local area and a new account executive to capture new business. I also began to support a number of local marketing specialists by contracting with them when my firm won larger than average projects. This model worked well because it allowed me to provide the best people for the job, and deliver a cost savings to my clients.

Become Customer Centered

With my new structure and team in place, my next move was to learn all I could about my customers. At this time my team is actively conducting surveys to gather information about the likes, dislikes, interest and marketing experience of individuals that fall into our key niche areas. Capturing this data will allow us to build our prospect database and be more effective at identifying and delivering the right solutions for the right people at the right time.

Final Thoughts

As you can see, implementing each of the actions above was not only helpful to the business; they also allowed me to make a much bigger contribution than I was at the time. Growth in these areas took time and some are still in process. However, the feeling of wealth I discussed at the beginning of this chapter has since returned and expanded. This sensation now permeates every cell of my body. It causes me to hear more sharply, see in brighter colors, sleep more restfully, and care more deeply for others. It has also increased my sense of confidence as an entrepreneur. This boost in confidence has given me the additional motivation and courage needed to take on larger, higher paying contracts which not only support me but also allows me to provide jobs and new opportunities for others.

My Now...

The Moral of this Story

As long as you "chase the deal" it will always out run you. When you stop chasing and relax into your success, by nurturing an attitude of gratitude, thinking of others and following a well laid plan, the waters of abundance will flow in your life more generously than you could have ever imagined.

...for the *Entrepreneur*

My Now...

...for the *Entrepreneur*

Ready, Aim, Fire

Anonymous Angel

NEVER TAKE ANYTHING YOU PERCEIVE AS COMMON SENSE FOR GRANTED.

NEVER.

If anyone tells you, "Never say never!" recall this story and ignore them. Sometimes, it's RIGHT to say "Never!"

Picture ten military, retired, most with at least the rank of Lieutenant (Rank changed to protect the innocent and prevent anyone from trying to figure out who the story is about....) All of the individuals from various .mil groups, various successful projects, missions, etc., but now retired and used by the government to train some of the new kids. Various training programs, various requirements, various times, various reasons, because of various specialty skills. All originating humans honorable, with awards on exit from their original commissions. All very involved and respected in their community. A strongly loyal group, forged by common history, common goals, and common training. You get the picture.

So, they set off, at the request of the home office, to do some chores. They stood up an entire program for on-demand training assistance. Along the way, each had their swim lanes created, responsibilities defined, and everything was going smoothly. Five years and running, the program was given awards, provided accolades, multiple .mil groups requested their help. Collaborations all around. The project expanded based on the number of consistent successes, scores of students coming home with written recommendations to go through this program, as 'it saved our lives.' A great success...

Until, one day, five years into the program, within a four-day stretch, 27 text messages were sent by one of the trusted trainers, to a customer, with strenuously negative comments about another customer.

Notice the carefully worded sentence from beginning to end. Re-read every section, and let it sink in.

After five (count them, 5) years of success, one incident crashed the program. And here is the list of 'NEVER!' commands:

1. NEVER assume that your employees have automatically trained themselves on how to engage with a customer.

...for the Entrepreneur

2. NEVER avoid a training session with employees, because you ASSUME they know how to act with the customer.

3. NEVER disengage and assume all the employees are doing well and that because they have a history of competence and professionalism, that they haven't experienced something that puts them (and you) in jeopardy.

4. NEVER forget to stay in close touch with whatever programs you have going, and if you personally can't, make sure someone you trust is watching over and supporting those that are facing the mega stress environments we all face in business today.

5. NEVER let anyone's personal life slip through the cracks, without a back-check, so you can support and head off incidences from even occurring.

BECAUSE:

Based on the aforementioned activity, the individual that cracked and lost his professionalism was demanded off the job immediately. Not an unreasonable request.

Based on that individual's behavior, the entire team was then called into question.

My Now...

Based on that individual's destruction of the customer trusted relationship, in the middle of a Response to a Request for Proposal for work the follow-on year, the customer reviews determined that the entire team was no longer the same quality that they had trusted all the previous five years. And, exactly that fast, the entire program was turned over to a different group. Not only did the remaining nine (9) training staff end up out of work, with the turn over to the new group came an inconsistency in the end result, and people down range were put in danger. Training program halted. One single person changed the stream of excellence.

Within 24 hours, four upper management humans were standing in a room with little to say except: "What the heck just happened?" "How did we miss that he was coming unglued?" "Who would expect anyone of his caliber to do anything so stupid?" "Did you know he was....?" So many unanswered questions.

From lessons learned, in order of the "NEVER" list above, here are the action responses to each item:

1. Spend time with each employee as they come through the door, setting clear expectations as to what communications with customers should be, and how they should be presented. Set limitations on communication styles. Educate them on how you expect them to present themselves for the benefit of the company. Not everyone is

your friend, and not everyone sees your text messages, emails or sarcastic humor the same. Exercise caution and professionalism, and if they haven't been trained, provide it. Every company has a different culture. As they migrate into yours, help them be successful in transitioning to your company/customer's language specifics.

2. Even if an employee has some history with a customer, reminders on how to create customer perceptions are important. Monthly emails? Professional growth seminars? Who knows what's right for your company, but don't let this go because you think all humans have been exposed to the requirements of business relationships. Not all companies are raised on golf and beer sessions!

3. Always check in with employees as often as possible. Find out how they're doing. How? ASK THEM!!! Basic conversations with the humans that are helping create your future is a critical skill. Watch them as they're talking to you. Are they comfortable? No? WHY???

4. I recommend at a minimum weekly reviews with program staffers. Not just a five-sentence written email, i.e., "...the customer asked for... it will cost.... $...." That's all a math function. Easy day. How does the customer react to your humans? How do your humans view your customer? How do they interact with them? What's happening in each of their worlds that would predict a change in how business is

My Now...

run? One person's sour attitude, on one off day, can affect how a lower-level staffer on the customer side of the project provides feedback up the chain to the check writers. Have you helped your people learn how to converse with good and bad customers?

5. And here is the last, most important section: As you get to know your employees, and you run into any issues, always ask five 'why's.'

1. Why did this happen?
   a. Why did that happen?
      i. Again, why?
         1. Why? Etc.
            a. Why?

For each of the 'why's' you ask, you should be learning whether or not it is a systemic problem within your company that created the issue, or whether the employee has underlying cause/effect issues. The 'problem' may not be the employee; it could be lack of attention to detail by the company. Here we go with this specific circumstance's set of 'why's:'

Q: Why did the employee send the text messages?

A: The customer created an unsafe situation, which actually threatened the life of a fellow customer/student. Bad venting on part of trainer.

...for the Entrepreneur

Q: Why did the customer/student create the unsafe situation? What happened?
A: The customer/student didn't follow the safety drill of .... (performance of a specific physical action)
Q: Why did the customer/student not follow that safety drill?
A: Not enough sleep, forgot.

Q: During a training week, why not enough sleep?
A: Stayed up all night off site, drinking....

Q: Aha. And who was there? Why weren't the students back at bunk?
A: The trusted trainer was with them.

Q: Really. And, why was the trusted trainer out with the student?
A: Student/Customer invited, Trainer thought it was ok, ended up being all nighter, talking about old times on the job. Company never prohibited trusted trainer from socializing with customers.

In this case, followed to six questions, didn't stop at five. What was learned?

The answer to Why's? Multiple:

1. Company didn't educate the employee on the prohibition of socializing with the Customer, Trainer never even blinked at the invitation, actually thinking it would be a good activity for future business.

My Now...

2. HOWEVER, unknown to the company, the Trainer had a long-term battle with alcohol, so the following morning was surly and caustic, changing the atmosphere of the class entirely; thus, the nasty text messages. Additionally,

3. When the Trainer made a joking derogatory comment about lack of safety the 'tired' customer/student to another 'student,' he was unaware of the personal relationship between the two students. VERY poor judgment, not counteracted because of lack of training, line Item #1.

Can you imagine how fast that all spun out of control?

Fault? Company. No expectations or prohibitions were set, nothing ever discussed on this subject, employee had positive motivation (benefit of the company), but misguided. Or, should we say, NON-guided!

Fault? Company. Didn't know the employee well enough to discern that there was an issue the employee might encounter, and no guidelines set that would help the employee be successful, by avoidance.

Fault? Company. By not knowing/doing the foregoing, or even setting up basic training within their own company, they inadvertently also damaged the training of the end customer, putting lives at risk with whom they had no contact. Their critical knowledge and history, that could

...for the *Entrepreneur*

have contributed to the well-being of others was boxed up and put away.

The unintended consequence of cutting corners can have far reaching effects. The end result goes far beyond the newly bad reputation of the individual employee. It can brand an entire company, and change the future of those that depend on their expertise.

This is a very strong example, and not intended to have a negative impact. It is a true story, provided to tattoo on your memory why the various sections of the story are salient to ANY company:

1. Success or failure of any project or any company rests in the details of functionally interacting with multiple types of humans on multiple levels.

2. This is NEVER a linear process. (Yes, there's that word again, strenuously emphasized, emphatically!)

3. It is often difficult for linear thinkers to be successful in managing a company, because they don't realize how multi-layered successful system thinking processes are.

4. And then there is that pesky Human Factor. Not every great employee has been exposed to all facets of business management or survival. Don't set your own expectations up for failure.

My Now...

5. NEVER (repeat aforesaid 'emphatically') assume that any of your Humans can read your mind, or that they have been exposed to the same experiences you have. Share your experiences and failures, share your successes. Make sure you are an open door, and require at least three questions a day from everyone. You will learn more about the health of your company than you expected.

6. NEVER expect others to think the same way you do. In fact, EXPECT them to think differently. You hired them to fill in your cracks, remember? You will learn from them more about your inadequacies as a manager than you ever hoped, for sure. Take advantage of those learning opportunities.

7. And for the sake of peace in the castle, make every effort to teach them what they need to know to survive! Just because they can jump off an ice mountain and float for 300 feet does NOT mean they know how to talk to a customer and avoid drinking with them! Lead them to improved skills, don't negatively browbeat them. Great managers engender loyalty and followers, not refugees.

All the foregoing is just my humble opinion, based on working up through the ranks from secretary in 1977, transcribing the Watergate tapes, to owning three companies of various purposes. One of them is currently on the verge of failure, because of the foregoing story.

...for the Entrepreneur

Good luck has little to do with any of it.

Blood, Sweat & Tears does it all.

Anonymous Angel

My Now...

Sherontelle Dirskell

Sherontelle Dirskell known as, (Ms Slim) born and raised in Cleveland, Ohio. Sherontelle attended Ursuline College for undergraduate studies in Science. She is now recognized as Music Pr Professional who currently works as an Independent liaison between artist, labels, and media outlets. Her company founded in 2011 Ms Slim Promotions which focuses on social media marketing, media relations, and artist branding. "Bringing the Hottest Artists to the Industry" is her company motto. In this short three year span Ms Slim Promotions expertise in the above mentioned areas has afforded her the opportunity to work with independent artists to Multi-Platinum Grammy Winning Producer/Artists who has become industry icons and household names. Ms Slim Promotions approaches each project whether large or small with a passionate, detail-oriented disposition. Her company believes that every artist should be heard and given the opportunity to realize their dreams regardless of genre, budget, or technical savvy.

Msslimpromotions.com

Msslimpromos.blogspot.com

msslimpr@gmail.com

@msslimgdy

...for the Entrepreneur

Quiet Resilience

Sherontelle Dirskell

No One would have ever guessed that the little girl that lived in the brick house with her grandmother with the huge oak tree in front would own her own business. It seems just like yesterday that it would be the best thing to do when I was a child growing up is to finish high school, go to college, receive a degree and get the dream job that I've always wanted. In today's economy it really pushed me to think about moving in a different direction where I could have more freedom of a flexible schedule but trying not to focus so much on the financial gain I just wanted to do something that I would love doing and have fun doing it. I wasn't sure how I would get started or what I would have my business in. I always knew that I wanted to go out and get ready to set myself up for what is called my life journey.

One day I decided to start signing up with several different social media sites to start networking with people from all over the world until I could figure out what it was that I was going to do with my idea. When I take a look at other businesses that became successful all it took was an idea to

My Now...

build a business that can really change your life. So I came up with the idea that I would go into media relations. I did a self evaluation and thought it would be lots of fun since I definitely am a people person and I love to help others reach their goals I thought this would be the perfect industry to work in. One day I was on twitter and reached out to a Platinum R&B music Artist from my hometown Cleveland, Ohio I will keep his name anonymous. Based on my crazy work ethic that he had seen he gave me an opportunity to work with his company and be a part of his team in media relations. He truly acted as my business consultant and guided me with the direction that I needed to go to start my adventure. Having this opportunity gave me a chance to learn more about working in music industry.

As time passed by I was starting to feel as if I could start doing it alone. I continued to network and came up with a business plan and a name and decided to become independent in music public relations. My fear is what led to this decision. When I first started I was so afraid of losing and wondering where I was going to get my clients from. Fear has always been my motivation to do what others would say would be impossible to do. I am from an urban neighborhood in Cleveland, Ohio. I was never really exposed to what success was nor was I doing anything that would help me grow as an individual. If I dreamed too big, I was told that it couldn't happen; to look around and stop dreaming. Telling me to stop dreaming is like saying I should just die. My Faith in God is so strong that I knew there was nothing in this world that I couldn't do. When I make a goal I just go after it and consider it already done. I live to work and love to be challenged. I mentally prepare myself for the challenges through prayer, meditation and yoga. Doing these things has been my balance because I learned over the years that the only way to be truly successful is have happiness.

Once I had started my business, I immediately started feeling the fear rise again because I didn't want to fail. I let my fear be my motivation to win; I was determined to tune out all of the naysayers the people that said I couldn't do it. I had to listen to that whisper inside of me that said I could do it, my determination; I had to have a crescendo of self encouragement. So I put the fear aside I was ready and willing to take risk, I stopped focusing on loss, never expected an overnight success and start giving up a lot of my time for free no financial gain. I just wanted to be a part of others careers and help them win and it also gave me an opportunity to build my contact list. I was aggressive in a charming way and always took no as a great way to know I was on my way to hear "Yes". My losses kept my failures small because for the first year of starting I made no money, but I made a long list of contacts based on all the networking that I was doing and to me that was worth more than any check that I could have ever received but I also knew that I

My Now...

needed to start charging for my services but I love what I did so much I felt guilty for charging money. Starting my business was the first step, building has been a continuous process and maintaining it through all my oppositions has been a part of my success.

Usually if someone becomes a Music Pr they would work for a Firm or huge company. I just never had the desire to do so; I always wanted to have the challenge of building and getting the press on my own and being more one on one with my client. I grabbed as many books as I could to have continuous learning and continued to network and get help from friends who had been in the business a lot longer than I had so I could be one the best music Pr in the business. I have been most inspired by my great friend and also client Bernard Edwards Jr. known as Grammy Winning Producer Focus formerly of Dr. Dre's Aftermath Entertainment. He believed in me when I first start working on my own public relations. Working with someone so humble such as he taught me how important it is to have people around me that are positive and are just as excited as I am about my goals. It would definitely be fair to say he has been a great Mentor having a listening ear when business gets stressful for me and sharing lessons and life experiences to help get me through. I found that in life you have to surround yourself with positive people so that it balances the negatives ones. Focus has truly been a huge blessing in my life and I have learned so much from him and thank God for the opportunity to work with someone

...for the Entrepreneur

that is so humble such as he. Since I've started public relations I have build a portfolio of countless contacts, have worked with so many great talents and humbled to say that I have recently been doing some public relations for R&B singer, actor, author and model Tyrese.

One of the biggest parts of building my business has been networking and building healthy working relationships. Continuously keeping myself surrounded with those that have positive energy and making sure that I keep in touch with my personal life coach and mother figure Mary Ellen Dale, Ph.D. It's so important for me to be able to keep my life balanced. I celebrate my success and evaluate my weaknesses.

Going through my life journey I have had my fair share of life oppositions from being to a survivor of domestic violence, single parenting, string of broken relationships, losing friends through death and tragic accidents and being able to leave the economic pitfalls of living in Cleveland, Ohio. My quiet resilience has been overcoming my insurmountable obstacles and maintaining a peace of mind. Every scar of each tragic event I have been through has only been fuel for the compassion I pour into my projects for each of my clients I can remember having so many stressful nights working with little sleep but my love for helping others win surpass my sleep deprivation. My day would start with about three hours of sleep and a large cup of coffee to get me through the day. I would start with hundreds of emails and phone calls. As time

My Now...

went on I had to start making better choices of how I would work towards meeting my goals.

Not everyone was interested on every project that I was working on so I had to keep an open mind to prepare myself for those people who would be so rude to me and stay focused on what I was trying to accomplish. I had to remain consistent and stay focused on the fact that I believed in my campaigns and I wouldn't let that detour me because I was always on a mission to see my projects succeed. I definitely describe myself as a workaholic and I live by the model the more hours that I put into working and staying up late the more successful I would be. I'm always, constantly, reinventing myself. Yet still to this day I can't find any other way to put in countless hours to my craft of promoting, preparing press releases and numerous emails and phone calls I learned that I needed to make sure that I get enough rest and eat healthy so that I was ready for whatever day was coming my way. My hard work and sleep deprivation has been my personal recipe for success. I never make a Plan B because I feel if I set out to do a task it must be done by any means necessary. I put my whole heart and soul into my projects because I absolutely enjoy everything about public relations. I have been willing to do whatever it takes to make my dream come true. My goal has been to definitely set the bar high and to become the next Music Public Relations Mogul. I don't believe that I will ever have a goal that will make me feel like I'm done because I feel like goals

...for the Entrepreneur

are a continuous projects I complete one then I prepare to start another one.

No one every told me and I never prepared myself for what happens when you do reach a certain level of success. My expectations of my friends and family were very high. Sadly mistaken I set myself up for a true heart break. I found that I was losing people that I thought were my friends very quickly. I have such a great love for my friends they would be there cheering for me and supporting all the great things that were happening for me. Through my quiet resilience I've learned to not feed into the negativity and look at the big picture and say to myself that I must me doing something right if people are starting to take notice of me. I now just keep the circle of close friends and family that truly love and support what I do with no expectations. I'm able to overcome those that don't support me by having self-control and having my spirituality, with my Love for God and knowing what my true purpose in life is.

The moment I decided to accept my past, my flaws, and all circumstances rather they were good or bad that's when I knew I was ready to take my goals to the next level. I had to keep living to realize that my past was just that and it had nothing to do with my ability and potential to turn my life into something beautiful. Balance, peace, and my well-being has been my success. The ability to continue to strive despite all of my oppositions has opened up doors to limitless

My Now...

opportunities. I am an entrepreneur at heart I feel like I have been destined and born to do what I do. No longer afraid to face my fears, willing to take risks, I have hope, optimism and future-minded.   Life is just a capsule of time and what I do with my time means the world to me. I feel like my purpose in life is to help others achieve their success. As I continue to move forward I ask God to give me strength to continue to use these talented gifts he gave me and to stay connected with my spirituality. I'm taking it one day at a time but so excited on what's to come next on this journey.

...for the *Entrepreneur*

Books by Moovin4ward Publishing

- **My Vision, My Plan, MY NOW:** Motivation You Need to Take the Action You Want

    By Moovin4ward Authors

- **Mapping Your Journey to Success**: Six Strategies for Personal Success

    By Sharon A. Myers & Mark W. Wiggins

- **Slumber Party,** A story of four girls who pledge to survive high school and life... but didn't.

    By Sharon A. Myers

To book a certified Moovin4ward speaker to present a program, email speakers@moovin4ward.com

To purchase any Moovin4ward books in bulk at discounted rates, email books@moovin4ward.com.

www.Moovin4ward.com or www.Journey2SuccessPSSP.com.

www.ingramcontent.com/pod-product-compliance
Lightning Source LLC
Chambersburg PA
CBHW060513090426
42735CB00011B/2206